HARLEY-DAVIDSON
CHRONICLE

BY DOUG MITCHEL

Publications International, Ltd.

ISBN: 0-7853-1682-5

Library of Congress Catalog Card Number: 96-67107

Photography

All photos in this book by **Doug Mitchel,** except those credited to
Harley-Davidson and the following:
Tom Perkins, Noel Paraninfo, Scott Barber: 40, 49; **Phil Toy:** 152,
153; **Wallace Salley:** 219: **Michael Kan:** 126, 282; **Mark
Leivdal/Shooting Star:** 316; **C.W. Bush/Shooting Star:** 316;
Michael Ferguson/Globe Photos: 316; **Janet Gough/Celebrity
Photo:** 317; **Albert Ortega/Celebrity Photo:** 317; **Mark
Weiss/Angles:** 317; **R. Price/Alpha/Globe:** 317; **Fitzroy
Barrett/Globe:** 317

Owners

Thanks to the owners of the motorcycles featured in this book for
their enthusiastic cooperation. They are listed below, along with
the page number(s) on which their bikes appear:

**Special thanks: Rev's Vintage Rides, Temple City, CA;
Paul Pfaffle, Vintage Classics, Waukesha, WI; Rex Barret.**

Lynn Sweet, Harley-Davidson Museum, York, PA: 11, 60, 70, 125,
158; **Dave Kiesow, Illinois Harley-Davidson, Berwyn, IL:** 12, 13,
22, 23, 58, 59, 76, 77, 78, 79, 108, 109, 146, 147, 212, 213, 220, 221,
232, 233, 242, 243, 252, 253; **Henry Hardin Family:** 16, 17, 46, 47,
120, 121; **Bud Burnett, Bud's Harley Davidson, Evansville, IN:**
20, 21, 66, 67, 110, 111, 196, 197, 240, 241; **John E. Olberg:** 28, 29;
Dale Walksler, Wheels Through Time Museum, Mt. Vernon, IL:
18, 19, 31, 50, 51, 52, 54, 55, 60, 64, 65, 75, 80, 81, 89, 93, 96, 98, 99,
100, 101, 102, 103, 105, 113, 114, 115, 117, 126, 127, 130, 131, 133,
144, 145, 150, 168, 172, 173, 209, 248, 249, 258, 259, 282; **Pete
Bollenbach:** 34, 35, 282; **John Parham:** 36, 37, 41, 164, 165; **Mike
Lange:** 40; **Bob McClean:** 42, 43, 246, 247; **Tom Baer:** 44, 45, 62, 63;
Jim Kersting, Kersting's Harley-Davidson, North Judson, IN: 56,
57, 113, 117, 118, 119, 122, 123, 132, 187, 229, 234, 235, 245, 250, 263,
264, 265, 283; **Ray Schlee:** 82; **Paul Ross:** 86, 87, 214, 215; **Henry
Hack:** 90, 91; **Al & Pat Doerman:** 106, 107, 182, 183, 216, 217;
David Monahan, Perfect Timing Inc.: 128, 129, 140, 141, 239;
Elmer, Kokesh Cycle: 138, 139; **Walter E. Cunny:** 142, 143; **Marvin
Bredemeir:** 148, 149; **Pablo A. Lopez:** 152, 153; **Frank DeGenero:**
154, 155; **John Archacki:** 156, 157, 160, 161, 188, 189, 200, 201, 210,
211; **Elizabeth Phillips:** 166, 167; **Don Chasteen:** 170, 171, 178,
179, 224, 225, 230, 231, 244; **William P. Dokianos:** 174, 175; **Steve
Schifer:** 180, 181; **Stewart Ward:** 184, 185; **Greg Lew:** 194, 195; **Ted
Moran:** 202, 203, 222, 223, 256, 257, 284, 285; **Robert Scott:** 204,
205; **Richard Cronrath/Peter Eiser:** 219; **Tom Gentner:** 226, 227;
Buzz Walneck: 236, 237; **Al Wallschlaeger:** 260, 261; **Rick
Bernard:** 266, 267; **John Kasper:** 276, 277; **Lake Shore Harley-
Davidson, Waukegan, IL:** 278, 279; **Claudio Rauzi:** 288, 289;
Heritage Harley-Davidson, Lisle, IL: 290, 291, 296, 297, 302, 303;
Lou Gerencer Harley-Davidson, Elkhart, IN: 295; **Larry Melvin:**
295; **Bill Stewart, American Motor Works, Wabash, IN:** 304, 305;
Dennis Ahrens: 308.

CONTENTS

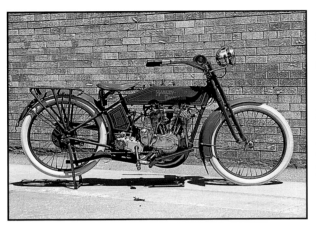

CHAPTER ONE

THE EARLY YEARS
(1903-1928)

Harley-Davidson grows from a backyard enterprise into the world's largest producer of motorcycles.

CHAPTER TWO

THE FLATHEAD IS BORN
(1929-1935)

The Great Depression weeds out many competitors, while Harley-Davidson manages to stay afloat.

CHAPTER THREE

THE KNUCKLEHEAD HITS
(1936-1947)

The overhead-valve Knucklehead engine is a monumental advancement that forms the basis for all future Big Twins.

FOREWORD

Motorcycle culture is unique in that it unites riders through aesthetic excitement as well as a sense of adventure. The design of Harley-Davidson motorcycles has consistently brought art and technology together, and the resulting machines are as exhilarating to look at as they are to ride.

There is a distinct American vision that Harley-Davidson has always brought into focus, and the approach to publishing this book successfully conveys the historical progression and inspired nature of the Harley-Davidson Motor Company.

The story of Harley-Davidson is always worthy of telling, but especially as a chronicle of the bikes themselves; for it is the machines that should be revered, not just the image they portray.

Harley-Davidson Chronicle depicts not only the history of the Harley-Davidson motorcycle, but the timeless heritage of the Company itself.

Dr. Martin Jack Rosenblum
Harley-Davidson Motor Company Historian

Some of the photographs in this book are from the Harley-Davidson Motor Company Juneau Avenue archives, and are identified as such within the text.

INTRODUCTION

The history of the motorized cycle began back in the late 1800s, yet even before the advent of the internal combustion engine, steam-powered cycles were on the scene. The first "motorcycles" were built in Europe, but the idea quickly spread to the States.

Once the powered bicycle hit U.S. shores, the race was on. No matter where you looked, someone was building their own version of the motorcycle. The formula seemed simple enough: Get a bicycle frame, install an engine, and sell them to the world. There was, however, a bit more to it.

By 1902, the Hendee Manufacturing Company was already building the now-famous Indian motorcycle out on the east coast, utilizing the same basic components that were seen elsewhere. Close on Hendee's heels were three young men who were toiling away in a small wooden building in Wisconsin.

William Harley joined with Arthur and Walter Davidson to construct the first Harley-Davidson motorcycle, which was finally rolled out in 1903. There was really no cutting-edge technology in the design, as they had simply brought together a single-cylinder engine (based on a DeDion design) and a tube-type bicycle frame. Painted in gloss black, that first machine was admired by friends and family—and that's where things started to get interesting.

After viewing the machine in action, several parties expressed an interest in buying one. Until that time, the boys had not given much thought to selling their creation commercially, but the following year, two gleaming motorcycles left their tiny factory. Trimmed by hand with the words "Harley-Davidson Motor Company" on the small fuel tank, they were truly handsome machines. In 1905, they recorded sales of eight motorcycles, and the number jumped to fifty units for 1906.

Seeing this new rage as more than a fad, William A. Davidson, eldest of the three Davidson brothers, joined the fledgling company in 1907. With his help, production rose to nearly 150 cycles that year, and the decision was made to incorporate the business.

As the Milwaukee company was growing, so was the interest in motorcycles. Manufacturers were popping up like weeds all across the country, and at the peak, it is estimated that there were nearly 300 different makes. Attrition would soon set in, however, with the numbers dwindling almost as fast as they had grown. But Harley-Davidson would prove to be a survivor—eventually, in fact, the *only* survivor.

Harley-Davidson had made a name for itself by producing strong, reliable motorcycles and selling them through equally strong and reliable dealerships. While the company enjoyed significant racing success in the late Teens, it wasn't speed that sold Harleys as much as reputation. Change came in slow, measured steps; engineering was rarely cutting-edge, but the bikes kept pace with contemporary technology while offering up a healthy serving of style and value.

Harley-Davidson Motor Company, Inc., continues on that same path today. With each passing year, new innovations and improved quality go into each machine that rolls out the door. Of course, like any large-scale manufacturing firm, the company has had its ups and downs. The acquisition by AMF in the late Sixties nearly ended the reign of the proud Harley-Davidson name entirely. But once taken back into the arms of a caring investor group, the chrome once again began to gleam brightly. Today, Harley-Davidson is a household word, and competitors are constantly striving to imitate the company's products. But try as they might, none will ever be able to duplicate the heritage that's an integral part of the Harley mystique.

THE EARLY YEARS

When William Harley and brothers William and Walter Davidson decided to build their own motorcycle in 1903, the result was rather typical for the period: essentially a bicycle powered by an engine based on a DeDion (of France) design. A large leather belt transferred power to the rear wheel, and starting was accomplished by strenuously pedaling the contraption until the engine sputtered to life.

Since modern mass-production techniques had not yet been instituted, each part of the 10.2-cubic-inch single was handmade. Sporting a vacuum-operated overhead intake valve and mechanical side exhaust valve, the little engine managed to churn out about two horsepower—enough to propel the crude machine at a brisk walking pace.

Though this would hardly seem a marketable mode of transportation, potential customers soon came a-callin'. A second prototype with a larger engine was built later that same year, and it was this machine that formed the basis for the early production versions. A grand total of two "Harley-Davidsons" left the factory the following year, and the boys from Milwaukee were in business.

Production soared to eight units in 1905, when the original factory was doubled in size—to 300 square feet. The next year brought a choice of colors: The traditional black was joined by Renault Gray, both being dressed up with hand-painted stripes. Output rose to 50.

Numerous motorcycle manufacturers were dotting the country by this time, but Harley-Davidson was earning a reputation as a builder of quiet, reliable machines. It was time to take the next step; one that would prove to be monumental for the fledgling company.

Now that motorcycles had proven to be a viable form of transportation, buyers began yearning for more. As one might guess (human nature being as it is), "more" meant greater speed—which in turn meant greater power. Enter the V-twin engine.

Introduced at a motorcycle show late in 1907, the first edition of "the engine that made Milwaukee famous" wasn't an altogether successful design. Still relying on inefficient vacuum intake valves and suffering from belt slip, the original production version introduced in 1909 lasted only a year. Taking a hiatus in 1910, the model returned with mechanically actuated intake-over-exhaust (IOE) valves and a belt tensioning system in 1911, and a legend was born.

With that, Harley-Davidson's technology began advancing at a rapid rate. The company introduced one of the industry's first clutches in 1912, chain drive became available in 1913, and a two-speed rear hub debuted for 1914, followed by a proper three-speed sliding-gear transmission the next year. Singles and V-twins were still offered, and while the former were more popular at first, they would eventually be phased out.

A rather odd fore-and-aft flat twin was introduced in mid-1919 but would last only four years. Meanwhile, the V-twin, which had grown from 50 cubic inches to 61 for 1912, was joined by a 74-cubic-inch version in 1921—the first of the famed "Seventy-fours."

A small-displacement single (21 cid) was introduced in 1926, offered in both side-valve (flathead) and overhead-valve configurations. More successful on the race track than in the showroom, these singles became known as "Peashooters" in reference to their exhaust note.

Strange as it may seem, flathead engines—the crudest of all four-stroke designs—were often considered superior to IOE or even overhead-valve configurations during this period. Though much of the flathead's popularity could be traced to easier servicing (something far more important back then than today), Harley decided it was time to adapt this valve layout to its V-twins, and the famous flatheads—due to survive for more than four decades—would replace the IOE engines as the Roaring Twenties drew to a close.

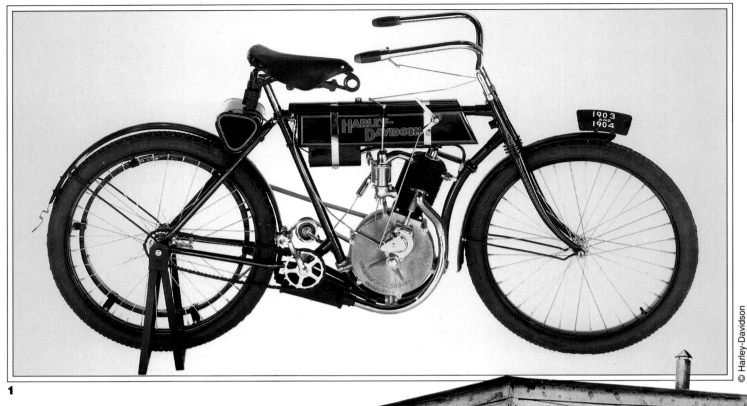

1. Though the first Harley-Davidson carried a little 10.2-cubic-inch engine that could propel it to little more than a fast walking pace, the second boasted a 24.74-cubic-inch engine that mustered up a reported 25 mph or so. Both might be considered prototypes; it was the later version upon which this early production model was based.

2. What is today the world-renowned Harley-Davidson Motor Company, started from very humble beginnings in Milwaukee, Wisconsin. William Harley teamed up with Arthur and Walter Davidson to finish their first motorcycle in 1903.

To 1903

The late-1800s see the birth of the motor-driven cycle in Europe

Americans discover the new machine and scramble to create versions of their own

The Indian Motorcycle Company, which would later become Harley's strongest competitor, is founded in 1901

The Wright brothers take flight at Kitty Hawk

The Ford Motor Company, which would also become a rival of sorts, is incorporated in 1903

The first post-season baseball series takes place

© Harley-Davidson

1

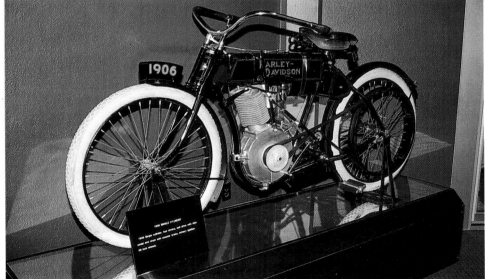

2

1. The first prototype used a slightly modified bicycle frame; the second prototype and early production models had a specially made frame with curved front downtube. 2. Harley's original paint scheme was black with gold striping, as evidenced by this 1906 model. That same year, however, Renault Gray was added as a color choice. 3. Steering head looks as though it came from a bicycle—and probably did. 4. Large handle beside the tank controls the belt tensioner pulley. 5. Tanks were hand-lettered.

3

4

5

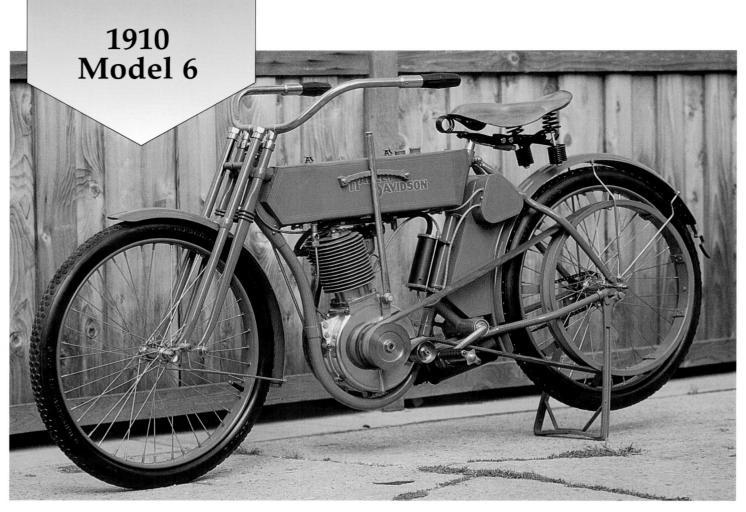

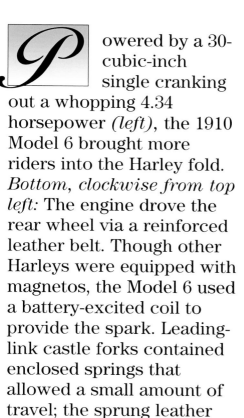

*P*owered by a 30-cubic-inch single cranking out a whopping 4.34 horsepower *(left)*, the 1910 Model 6 brought more riders into the Harley fold. *Bottom, clockwise from top left:* The engine drove the rear wheel via a reinforced leather belt. Though other Harleys were equipped with magnetos, the Model 6 used a battery-excited coil to provide the spark. Leading-link castle forks contained enclosed springs that allowed a small amount of travel; the sprung leather saddle handled suspension duties at the "rear." Carburetion looks crude today, but was far more sophisticated than on earlier models.

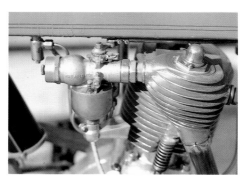

1

1. This group shot taken around 1908 shows William S. Harley sitting in the front of the sidecar, William A. Davidson sitting in the back of the sidecar, and Walter Davidson standing third from left. Missing is Arthur Davidson. 2. This famous photo hanging in the Harley museum depicts Walter Davidson Sr. after his victory in an endurance run in 1908. Inset shows the four founders standing in front of Harley Davidson headquarters in Milwaukee.

THE FIRST PRESIDENT, WALTER DAVIDSON, SR., AFTER HE WON THE FEDERATION OF AMERICAN MOTORCYCLISTS' ENDURANCE RUN IN 1908 WITH A PERFECT SCORE.

ARTHUR DAVIDSON, WALTER DAVIDSON, SR., WILLIAM S. HARLEY AND WILLIAM A. DAVIDSON DEMONSTRATED IN 1910 HOW THEY COMBINED TO MAKE SURE THERE WERE NO GAPS BETWEEN THE FRONT OFFICE AND THE SHOP.

2

1903 1904

Three young men in Wisconsin—William Harley and brothers Arthur and Walter Davidson—decide to try their hand at this new form of transportation, and their first motorcycle hits the streets of Milwaukee in 1903

Later in 1903, a second Harley-Davidson with a larger, smoother engine is built and becomes the prototype for early production versions

In 1904, works starts on the Panama Canal; construction would take 10 years

Theodore Roosevelt is elected U.S. president

1

2

3

1. By 1909, companies were realizing the value of motorcycles as delivery vehicles. 2. This happy young man is standing beside a 1909 Harley. 3. Another enthusiast—wearing a Harley-Davidson turtleneck no less—is set to mount his 1911 single. 4. The romanticism of motorcycling was not lost on period authors. *Tom Swift and his Motorcycle*, published in 1910, was one of a series of Tom Swift adventures. 5. *Motorcycle Chums* was another series, each book placing the heroes in different parts of the country.

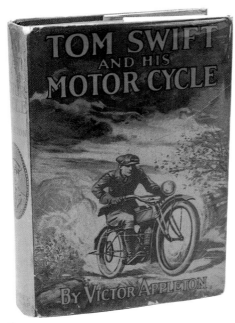

4

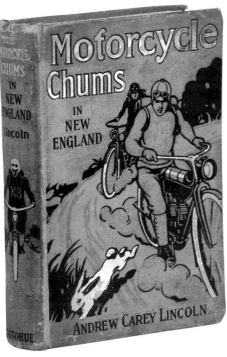

5

Though Harley's V-twin was back on the market after being discontinued for 1910 to fix some problems, singles still made up the bulk of sales in 1912. This X8A is powered by a 30-cubic-inch single driving the rear wheel through a leather belt. A belt-tensioning lever was mounted at the center of the fuel tank *(right)*. Behind that was a lever to activate the new Free Wheel Control, one of the industry's first clutches, which was contained in the rear hub. Pedals were still required to get the engine started. *Opposite page, bottom:* The single-cylinder engine *(left)* still made use of a vacuum-actuated intake valve, but was fired by a magneto *(center)*. An early Harley "coat of arms" appeared on the oil tank *(right)*.

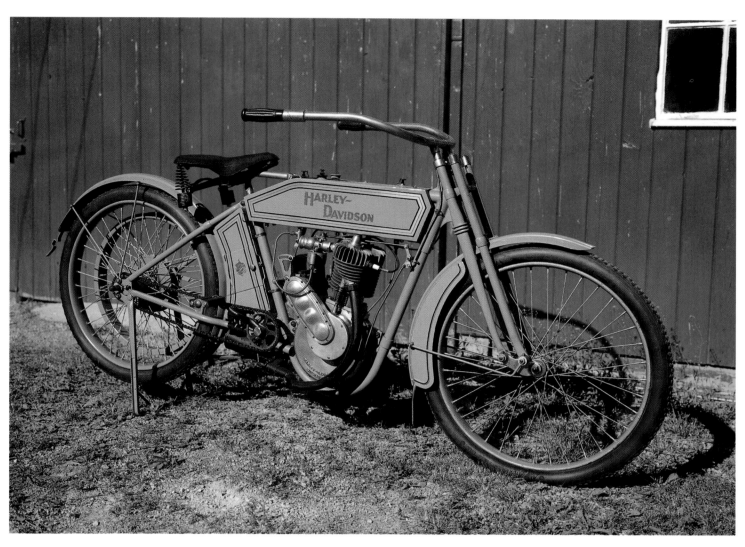

By the time this 1914 Model 10C was built, Harley-Davidson offered chain final drive, which was much more positive in operation than the old leather belt. The 35-cubic-inch single put out five horsepower with the help of a new mechanical intake valve. Front suspension *(above)* still provided only limited travel. *Top left:* The clutch could be activated by either a hand lever or foot pedal. *Bottom, clockwise from left:* Speedometer, mounted atop the tank, was driven by a gear set from the rear wheel. A small plunger at the bottom of the oil tank allowed the rider to pump more oil to the engine under severe use.

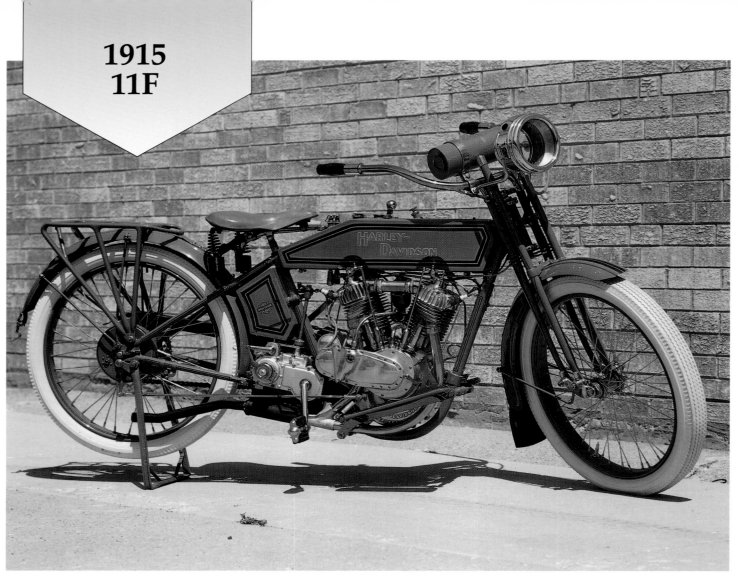

everal new features were offered on Harley V-twins for 1915, including a three-speed transmission with tank-mounted shifter *(opposite page, lower left)*, and an automatic oiler that helped prevent under- or over-oiling the 61-cubic-inch V-twin *(lower right)*. Electric lighting was also available, but many riders had more faith in the old acetylene system *(this page, top)*. Suspension systems remained rather primitive, but riders of the day were easily pleased; they were happy to get this sprung leather saddle *(middle)*. Pedals were still included, but floorboards had been added for 1914.

1904
1905
1906

1904 sees two Harley-Davidsons built and sold

William Harley leaves to get engineering degree

The following year, eight Harleys go to eager customers

With production in full swing, the 1906 total comes to an impressive 50 units

Louis Lumiere develops color photography

Color choices double for 1906: the original black is joined by Renault Gray

Quiet running and the new gray paint soon prompt the sobriquet "Silent Gray Fellow."

© Harley-Davidson

1

Opposite page: 1. The young man in the center looks proud of his 1911 Harley-Davidson single. 2. Women were not unknown pilots during that time. Note the tandem seat. 3. Though not dated, this employee photo would appear to be from around 1910, as the single-cylinder engine being displayed on top of the box at left seems to be from that era.

2

This page: 1. The men whose names were on the building. From left to right: William A. Davidson, oldest of the Davidson brothers who joined the company in 1907; Walter Davidson, Sr., who successfully raced early models; Arthur Davidson, who started building the first motorcycle and actively recruited dealers; and William Harley, his partner, who in 1904 went off to the University of Wisconsin to earn an engineering degree. 2. A cigar-chomping rider stands beside his Harley single circa 1913. 3. Now this is a hearty couple.

© Harley-Davidson

3

23

1. Those too young to ride their own machines could still read about the adventure. This book, published in 1913, was one of a series. 2. This 1913 single is fitted with snow gear. The front wheel has its own ski, while an outrigger adds stability in the slippery stuff. 3. Arthur Mitchell, a noted racer of the period, stands next to his 1913 machine.

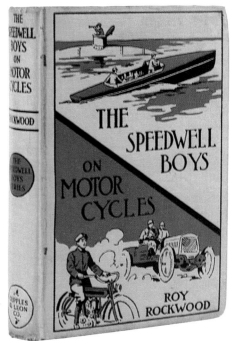

1

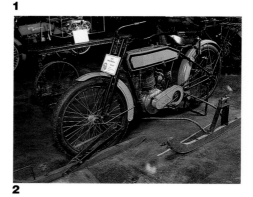

2

3

1907
1908

A third Davidson brother, William, joins the firm in 1907; the word "Inc." is added to the Harley-Davidson name

Walter Davidson is one of three riders (27 entrants) to make perfect scores in a Chicago to Kokomo race in 1907

Production numbers keep climbing as 150 new motorcycles are built

1907 models are first to have Sager-Cushion spring forks; prototype V-twin displayed at motorcycle show

Walter wins Federation of American Motorcyclist's endurance run in 1908 with perfect score. Production: 450

William H. Taft elected U.S. President

General Motors is formed

1

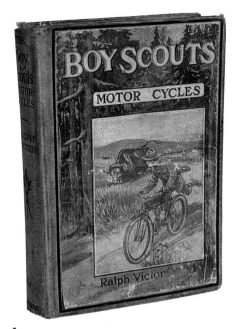

4

5

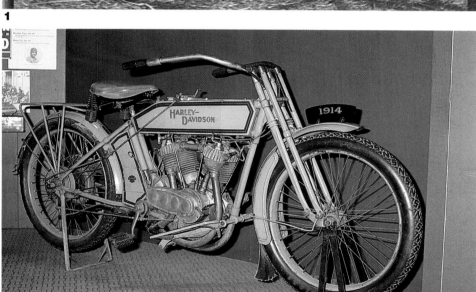

2

3

1. Barely able to reach the handlebars, this little tyke no doubt wishes he was big enough to ride this 1914 V-twin. 2. A similar bike is on display at the Harley-Davidson Museum in York, Pennsylvania. 3. This drawing depicts a foreign soldier riding a 1913 Harley. 4-6. These books represent just a few of the titles aimed at the young motorcycle enthusiast in the early Teens. *At the Front* was one of a series of adventures experienced by *The Big Five Motorcycle Boys*.

6

𝒫rior to 1916, Harley-Davidson assigned its bikes a model designation that started with a number representing the year of production minus four, since actual production didn't start until 1904; hence a 1915 motorcycle carried a designation beginning with 11. That changed in 1916, when designations were altered to coincide with the year of production, so the number was often dropped. This T model is a production racer built with a special high performance engine, denoted by its exposed exhaust-valve springs. The pedals identify it as having a single-speed transmission (those with the three-speed transmission had a "step starter" pedal only on the right), and it carries acetylene lighting. It lacks the decorative striping applied to regular production bikes.

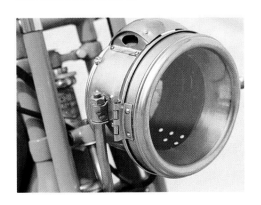

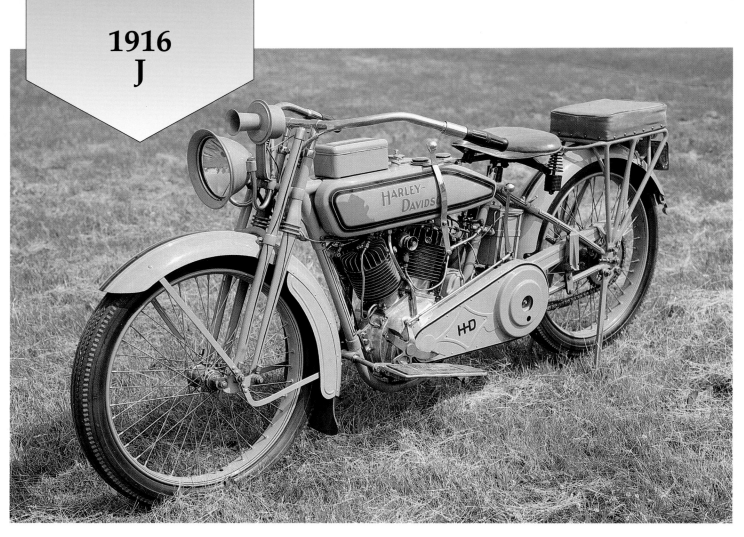

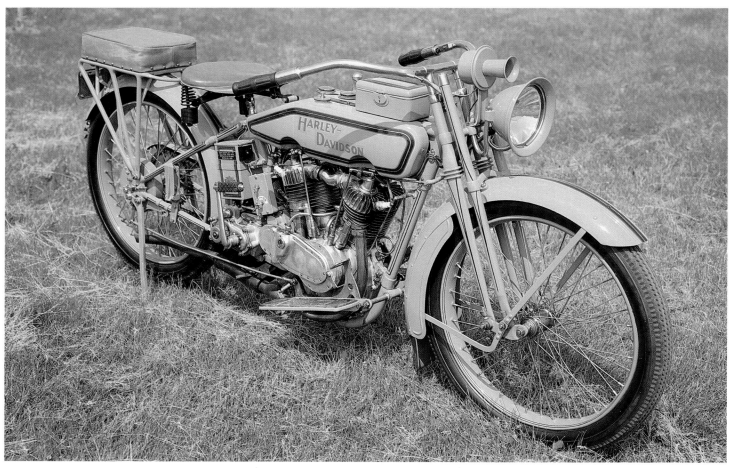

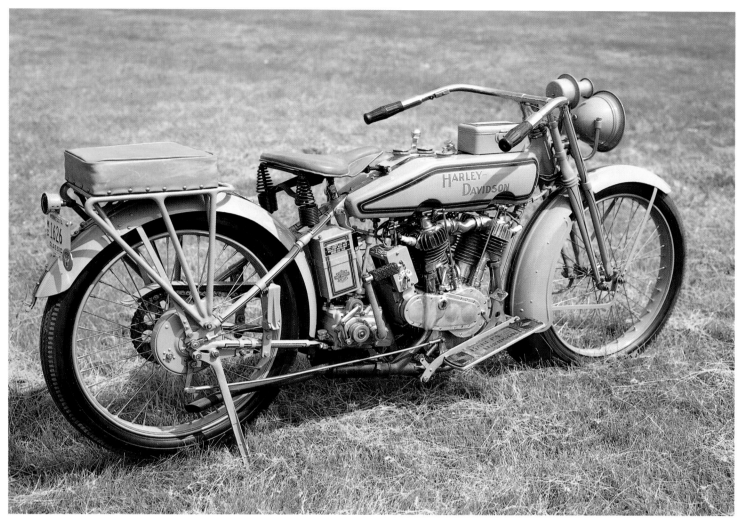

Stylistically, the 1916 Harley-Davidsons were a great leap forward. Fuel tanks now had rounded rather than square-cut corners, and pedals no longer sprouted from the lower frame on models with the three-speed transmission (those models used a rear-stroke starter like a modern kickstarter). *Above, left to right:* By 1916, intake manifolds on V-twins had been curved to smooth the flow of the air/fuel charge into the cylinders. This example is fitted with electric lights, which became available the year before. The magneto, located behind the engine, was switched on and off with a key—no doubt an attempt to foil those who coveted a Harley-Davidson but couldn't afford one.

—and now Harley-Davidson Bicycles

In the same Beautiful Military Drab that marks the 1917 Harley-Davidson Motorcycles

FOR more than 15 years Harley-Davidson motorcycles have been successfully sold in constantly increasing numbers, until now enthusiastic dealers are handling the products of the great Milwaukee factories all over the civilized world.

The name Harley-Davidson has come to be associated with the very highest quality of material and workmanship. This is one reason why a very decided demand has sprung up for a bicycle of the same remarkable quality. Harley-Davidson dealers have pressed us time and again to market a bicycle that they could sell with the knowledge that it was up to the Harley-Davidson standard—a bicycle which they would know would stand up as other Harley-Davidson products have stood up in strenuous service.

So for 1917 there will be a line of Harley-Davidson bicycles that will eclipse, we believe, in genuine value, any line now on the market. There will be men's bicycles, ladies' bicycles, boys' bicycles and girls' bicycles, and they will be absolutely the finest we can offer. That is saying a good deal, but the bicycles will back up the statement.

Not a Single Detail has been Overlooked

Aside from the beautiful lines and fine finish of the Harley-Davidson bicycles, every detail both seen and unseen has had the most careful consideration. Finely adjusted steering head bearings and properly designed front forks have resulted in unsurpassed light steering qualities.

Sturdy hangers, well supported on carefully ground bearings, insure very easy running.

Equipment is in keeping with everything else. Rims, spokes, hubs, coaster brakes, saddles and tires are of the quality and finish you might expect to find on a Harley-Davidson bicycle.

Before entering the bicycle industry we have held off until we could market a type of bicycles that Harley-Davidson dealers could sell almost on sight. We believe we have this kind of a line.

If you have a friend thinking of purchasing a bicycle you will do that friend a distinct favor if you suggest that an investigation be made of the Harley-Davidson line of bicycles. We feel confident that the bicycles will speak for themselves—and that they will sell themselves.

Anyone interested in the Harley-Davidson bicycles our bicycle circulars from the [...]

A Harley-Davidson Surprise —The New "Master 17"

We want you to see this new motor perform. The first time you handle it the sensation will force itself upon you that the motor is running away with itself.

"Pep" is the one word which best describes its performance.

A giant in power, this motor has the "jump," "punch," "getaway," and that extra burst of speed that will make it the talk of the trade.

Such snap has never been built into a motor before.

Slowed down on a hill it will pull, and keep on pulling.

We believe this motor will outrun and output any other stock motor. We make this statement because

More speed—more power—faster getaway—increased flexibility—ability to run slower—more pulling power when running slowly—increased gasoline economy—lower motor temperature—more silent operation—all these extremely desirable superior points of performance have been attained through the following 1917 features:

High velocity non-condensing intake manifold.
Roller bearings on drive side of crank shaft.
Hardened and ground steel washer in flywheel to reduce friction.
Improved silent acting cams.
Ventilated intake housing cap.
Intake valves with 30 degree seats.
Longer intake valve stem guides.
Longer intake valve springs.
Intake valve lifter arms fitted with rollers.
Enclosed push rod springs.
More coils in exaust valve springs.
Larger carburetor air valve.
Three-point air valve spring tension adjustment to compensate for atmospheric changes.
New carburetor needle valve cam.
Larger auxiliary air shutter on carburetor.

the Harley-Davidson has won every big race of the past season, and each one of these contests has taught us something new about motor performance, and all of this experience has been built into the 1917 twin motor.

Every feature, every detail, every refinement which the Harley-Davidson engineers have incorporated into this model 17 twin motor to give it its extra burst of speed and additional ounce of terrific smashing power has actually given it additional life and added to its reliability and endurance qualities.

The new 1917 twin motor is the result of concentration on one ideal—to produce absolutely the best motorcycle motor possible to make, regardless of the cost of production.

1. Harley-Davidson sold bicycles for several years starting in 1917. This sales pitch was contained in a motorcycle sales brochure and highlighted the bicycle's "beautiful military drab" paint. 2. For 1917, Harley touted the features of the new "Master 17" engine, claiming that its "pep" made it feel like it was "running away with itself." 3. This pastoral camping scene graced the cover of Harley's sales book that year. How the rider got all that equipment—not to mention the canoe—to the sight remains a mystery. 4. Sitting astride a 1915 model, this young soldier appears to be the chosen escort for the officer seated in the sidecar.

1909 1910 1911	Ford Motor Company introduces the first Model T in 1908 as a 1909 model; 15 million would follow	Harley's first V-twin, displacing 49.48 cubic inches, is introduced in 1909	That same year, Arthur Davidson begins to develop a dealer network in the Northeast
	1909 sees new tank styling along with optional magneto ignition and wire-operated controls; gray is only color	V-twin is temporarily discontinued in 1910 to work out some bugs	V-twin returns in 1911 with mechanically actuated intake valves to replace inefficient vacuum-operated valves, and a belt tensioner to prevent slippage

1

2

3

1. If you had attended a dirt-track race in 1917, this is one of the machines you may have seen circling the track. 2. Note the "seat" strapped to the tank. Needless to say, rider comfort was not a high priority. 3. "Shorty" exhaust pipes may or may not have produced more power, but they most assuredly produced more noise.

1. This 1914 V-twin is well-equipped with sidecar, gas lighting system (fed by the large cylinder attached to the rear of the frame), and rear luggage rack. Floorboards debuted this year, as did a two-speed rear hub, an internal expanding-band rear brake, and enclosures for the exhaust valves. 2. A "Harley-in-the-box," as delivered to a dealer in 1917—"some assembly required."

| **1912 1913** | 1912 sees several changes: top frame now sloped downward at rear to lower seat height; sprung saddle is introduced; larger 61-cid twin is made available, the first H-D to get chain drive; V-twins add hand oil pump; rear-wheel clutch is incorporated for smoother take-offs | S.S. Titanic goes down on its maiden voyage in 1912

Woodrow Wilson elected to first of two terms | All models boast mechanical intake valves for 1913

The first drive-in gasoline station opens in Pittsburgh in 1913; prior to that, gas was commonly sold at hardware or general stores |

1

2

3

4

5

1. This photo of a Harley-riding couple is printed onto a decorative mat. 2. A similar mat shows two young ladies astride their Harleys. 3. Famous racer Leslie (Red) Parkhurst is depicted on this period postcard. 4. Four men have loaded down their early-Teens Harleys for a long journey—or a really big lunch. 5. Introduced in 1916, the Eight-valve V-twin engine boasted four overhead valves per cylinder—two intakes and two exhausts—in a hemispherical combustion chamber. Unfortunately, the exotic powerplant was only used for racing.

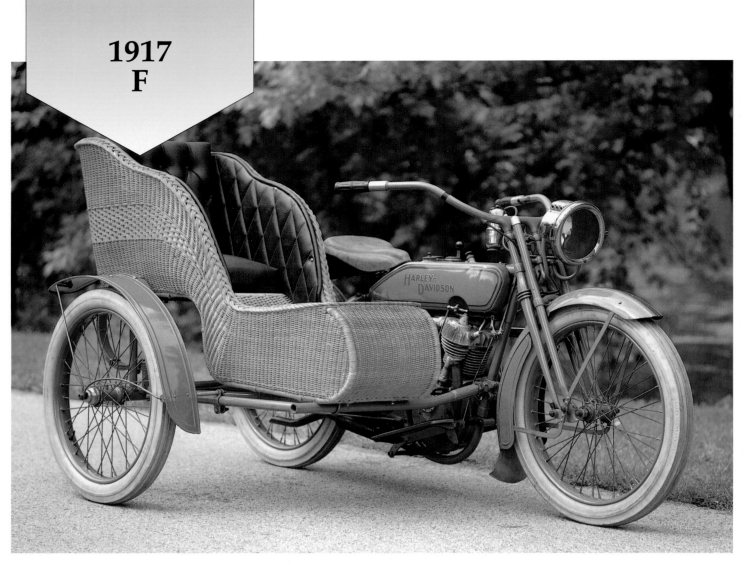

1917
F

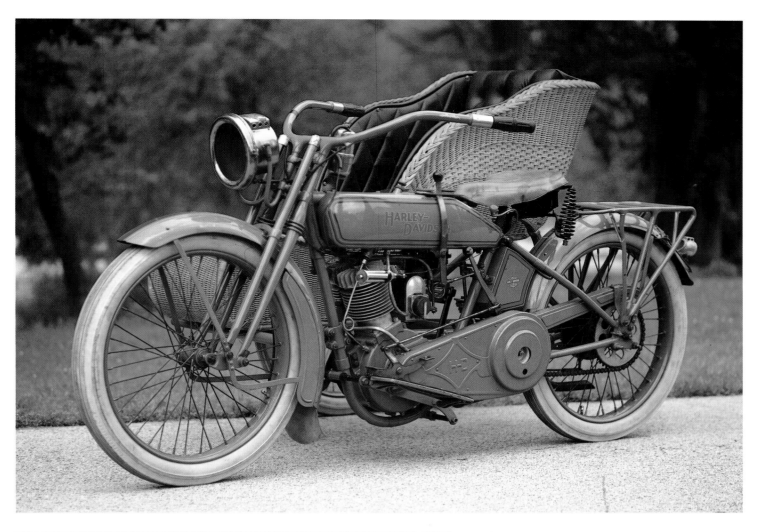

The biggest change for 1917 was a switch from gray to Olive Green paint, no doubt influenced by the war in Europe that the United States was about to enter. Though this Model F sidecar rig would seem to be underpowered with its single-cylinder "5-35" engine (five horsepower from 35 cubic inches), progress is aided by a three-speed transmission, whose shift lever sits beside the fuel tank. The angled lever below it is for the clutch, which could also be controlled with a foot pedal.

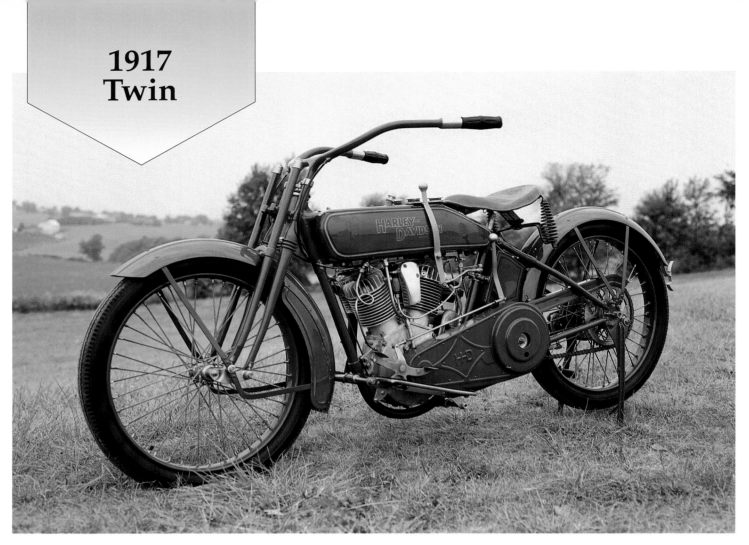

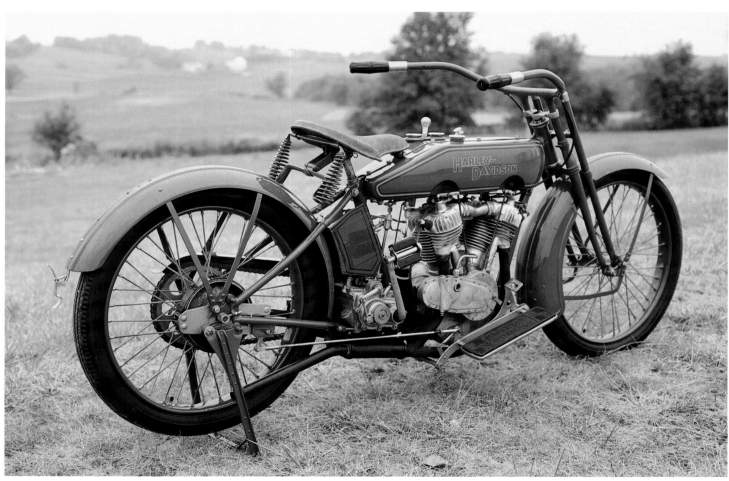

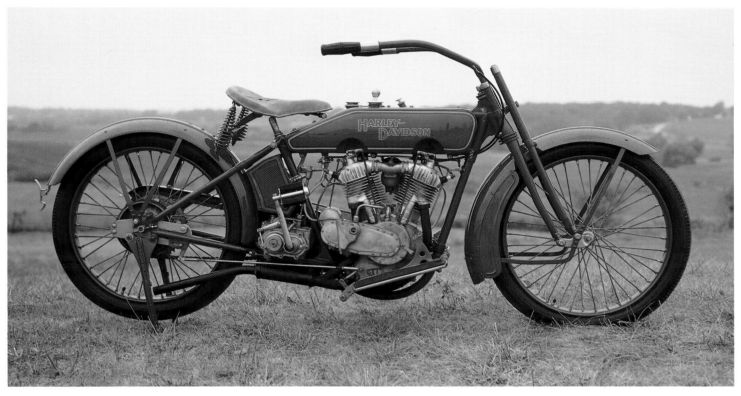

arley's F-head V-twins were improved for 1917 with the addition of the Eight-valve racer's four-lobe cam setup. Also for 1917, intake valve springs became enclosed, but only on the V-twins. *Top left:* The "fuel tank" had previously been split into two halves, the right side for fuel, the left side for oil. By 1917, the left side was itself split and now carried some of each—hence the three filler caps. *Top right:* Coaster or internal expanding-band brakes were used on earlier models with pedals, but external contracting-band brakes were added to bikes equipped with kick starters through the Twenties. *Left:* V-twins had kick starters in 1917, but singles still relied on pedals.

1

1. This dapper fellow—and his sidecar-riding family—appear to be participating in a local parade. 2. Harley's Eight-valve racing engines had been introduced in 1916, but only a handful were built. A couple of the last examples lacked exhaust pipes of any kind, the flames barking from the open ports providing a great show. 3. These two gents look ready for a ride over adverse terrain—either mud or snow. The man on the right is mounted on an Indian, but the Harley rider is apparently gracious enough to overlook that failing!

2

3

| **1914** **1915** **1916** | For 1914, the step starter is introduced; clutch and brake pedals are joined by hand levers; floorboards debut; two-speed rear hub is newly optional; internal-expanding rear brake joins external-contracting type | The company's manufacturing facility grows to nearly 300,000 square feet

Archduke Ferdinand of Austria is slain in 1914, igniting World War I

1915 brings a three-speed sliding-gear transmission, electric lighting, and an automatic oiler | First transcontinental telephone call goes from New York to San Francisco

1916: Fuel tanks are more rounded; two- and three-speed models get a kick starter while others still use pedals

Four- and eight-valve racing engines debut in 1916 |

1

2

3

4

1. A late-Teens Harley dealership displays lots of pedal-powered bikes but only a couple of the motorized versions. 2. Proving that he could use his motorcycle all year 'round, this gentleman has adapted skis and a homemade windshield to his bike, enabling him to take some friends on an undoubtedly slow—and cold— winter ride. 3. A suitor appears to be taking his best girl for a ride. 4. With spare tire at the ready, the open road beckons this circa 1915 traveler.

1

2

3

1917: U.S. enters war in Europe

Due to the war in Europe, 1917 Harley-Davidsons switch to patriotic Olive Green paint

Harley's company newsletter, "The Enthusiast," is first published in 1917, and offered free to the motoring public

Harley-Davidson becomes the world's largest manufacturer of motorcycles in 1918

Armistice signed by Germany in 1918; the "war to end all wars" ends

Influenza epidemic strikes; kills 22 million worldwide by 1920

Harley's factory race team earns the name "Wrecking Crew" as they consistently demolish the competition in the 1915–21 era

1

2

4

5

3

Opposite page: 1. San Francisco Harley dealer Dudley B. Perkins demonstrates his wares in a late-Teens hillclimb. 2. Championship racer Ralph Hepburn was depicted on a period postcard. 3. A private rider campaigned this unrestored 1915 single on the board-track circuit. *This page:* 1. Harley-Davidson sold bicycles alongside motorcycle in the Teens. This one's from 1919. 2. Harley pushed its single-cylinder models as the low-cost way to get around, but riders wanted power, not efficiency. 3. Hopeful future Harley riders play make-believe on a sidecar-equipped V-twin. 4. Harley bicycles wore a bronze badge on their steering heads. 5. This steel-toed boot cover was used by flat-track racers in the 1920s.

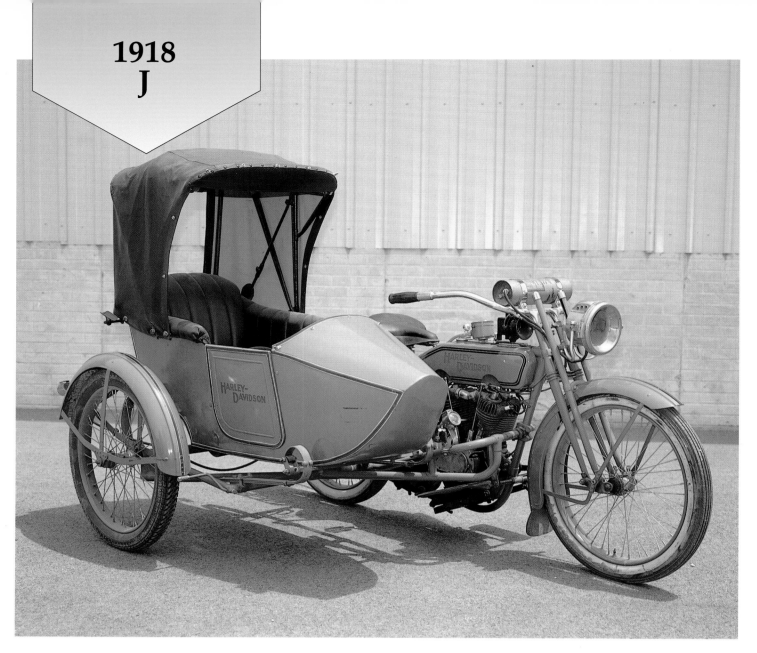

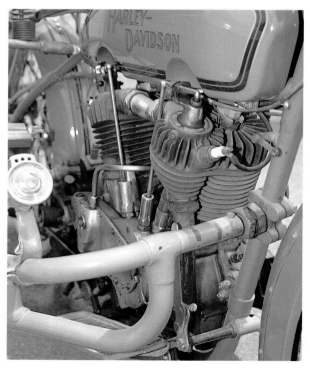

Harley's Model J was the most powerful and expensive motorcycle the company offered in 1918. It was well suited for use with the matching sidecar, which afforded its occupants more luxury—and better weather protection—than the motorcycle's rider. *Opposite page, clockwise from bottom left:* Staggered shifter gate for the three-speed transmission placed Low to the front, then Neutral, Second, and High toward the rear. Tank-mounted speedometers first showed up in 1915, and were driven by a gear on the rear wheel. Like the headlight, the taillight on this example was gas-powered. The tank holding the acetylene gas was conveniently fitted with a gauge (tank is mounted upside-down in this photo). Pressing down on the plunger activated the Samson Lion horn.

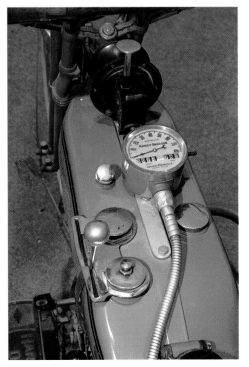

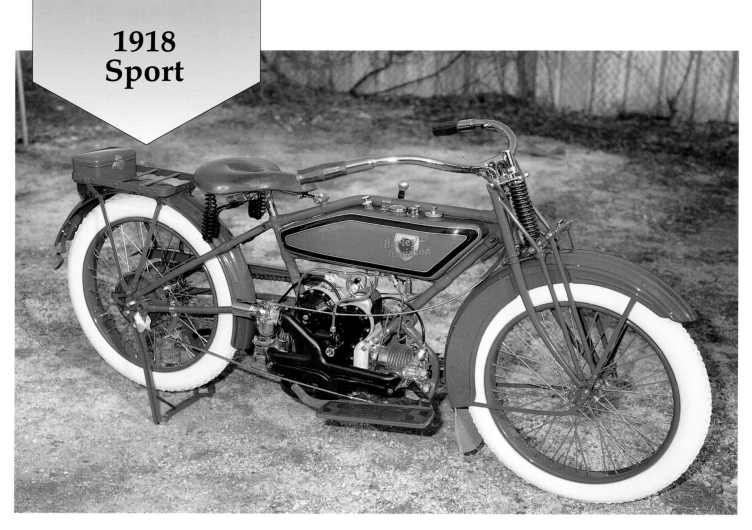

1918
Sport

44

A rather different approach for Harley-Davidson was the odd Sport model, introduced in mid-1919 to battle Indian's highly successful V-twin Sport Scout. *This page, top and bottom:* Harley's Sport was powered by a 35.6-cubic-inch horizontally opposed fore-and-aft twin driving through a three-speed transmission. *This page, center row, left to right:*

Despite its unconventional engine, the rest was traditional Harley: canister muffler, split (fuel/oil) "fuel" tank in Olive Green, and sprung saddle. The Sport failed to lure many customers away from Indian, and was dropped after 1923.

By 1920, only the Sport flat twin and 61-cubic-inch V-twin remained in the line. V-twin heads got round-edged cooling fins this year *(left)*, and headlights were positioned above the horn. Models with electric lighting, such as the motorcycle pictured, got Harley-made generators, and the battery box mounted atop the fuel tank carried an ammeter *(above right)*. Electric taillight *(above left)* also illuminated the license plate.

1. Brewster Green replaced Olive Green for 1922, but would last only two years. This 1923 V-twin sports the hinged rear fender introduced that year to aid in tire changes. 2. Though not identified as such, this appears to be a Harley-Davidson dealer's workshop, circa 1921. The famed 74-cubic-inch version of the flathead V-twin was introduced that year, as was a 37-cid single for commercial use.

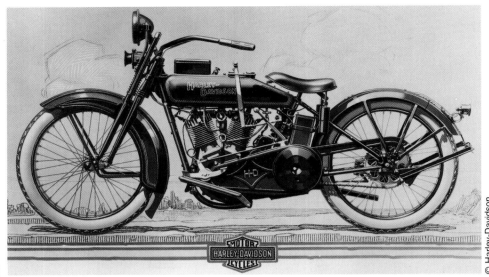

1

2

1919
1920

Only three-speed V-twins are initially offered for 1919, though a 35.6-cid flathead flat-twin Sport arrives at midyear

Jack Dempsey wins heavy-weight championship

1920: Sport gains electric lighting option; all late "electric" models are fitted with Harley-made generators and coils; headlight moves to above horn

Boston Red Sox sell Babe Ruth's contract to the Yankees for $125,000

Nearly 29,000 Harleys are sold in 1920, though a financial depression drives sales down by half the following year

1. Sport models gained electric lighting for 1920, while 1921 brought revised tank trim that more closely resembled that of the Big Twins. 2. Dudley B. Perkins Harley-Davidson opened its doors in 1914, and the San Francisco store is now the world's oldest Harley dealership. A banner announces the new 1922 models, while the front window advertises bicycles for Christmas giving.

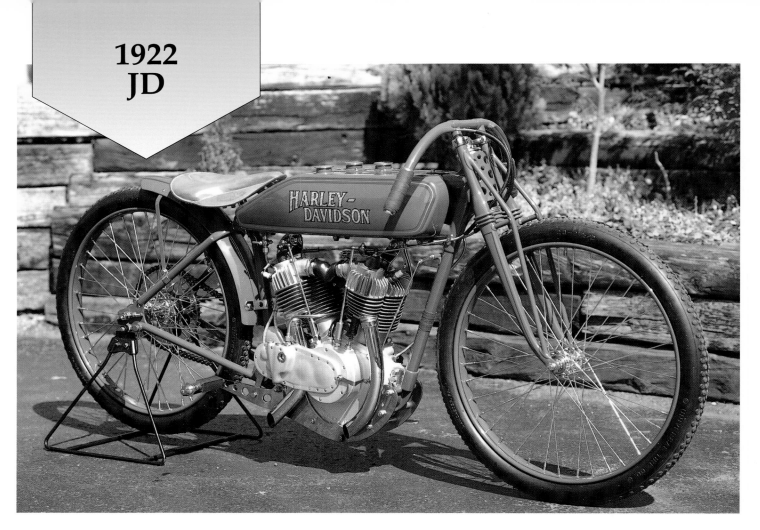

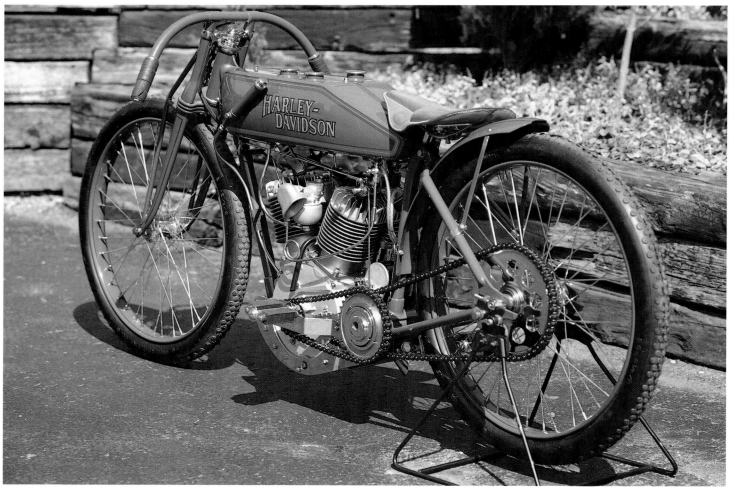

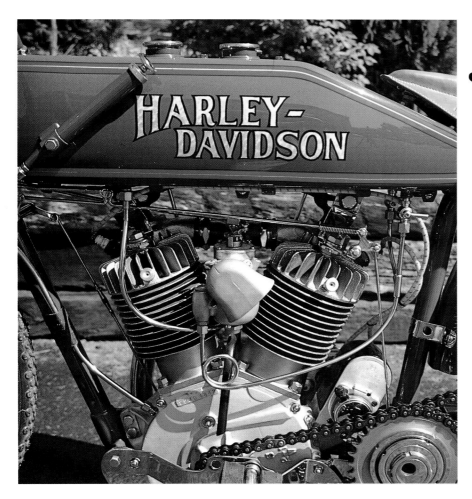

oard-track racing was very popular during the late Teens and early Twenties, and Harley's dominant factory racing team became known as the "Wrecking Crew." But by 1922, there seemed to be less correlation between winning on Sunday and selling on Monday, so factory support of racing was virtually dropped—at the peak of the team's success. This 1922 JD 61-cubic-inch board-track machine is typical of Harley's racing bikes of the era. It has no brakes, and precious little in the way of suspension: just a Merkel-style fork that moves up and down, compressing a spring inside the fork neck—allowing about one inch of travel.

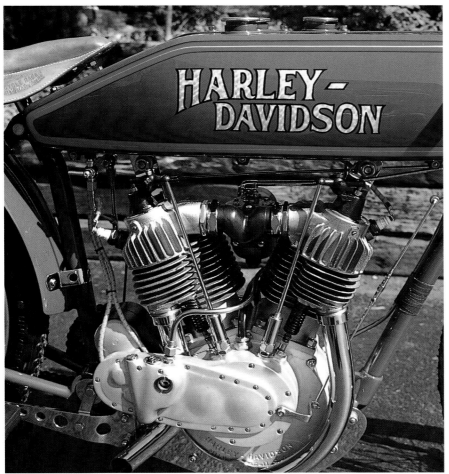

1. *The Enthusiast* has been published by Harley-Davidson since 1917.
2. A policeman stands next to his sidekick, a 1920 Harley V-twin. 3. Rider Carl Doran rode this board-track racer during the '20s. 4. Its engine carries special "Chicago" cylinders, which placed the spark plug nearer to the center of the combustion chamber. These engines were powerful but not very reliable.

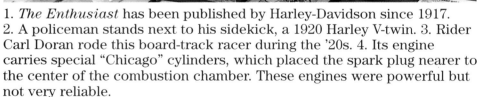

**1920
1921
1922**

1920: 18th Amendment added to U.S. Constitution, beginning Prohibition

Warren G. Harding elected U.S. president

A 74-cid V-twin debuts for 1921, though the 61-cid version is still available; front fenders gain leading-edge valance with concave section around forks

37-cid single added (half a 74 twin)

Company suffers its first operating loss in 1921 due to slow sales and recent expansion costs

Additional production space is gained by leasing shuttered breweries during the years of prohibition

1922: Factory rescinds racing support; Brewster Green replaces Olive Green

1. "Learn How to Ride in the Length of a City Block" was one of the virtues of the single-cylinder Harleys touted in this 1920s brochure. 2. These circa 1923 uniformed riders are likely police officers; note bowties, badges, and sidearms. 3. With graphics that read "Harely," this wind-up toy was popular in the Twenties, and still is today. 4. Another wind-up toy of the 1920s, this one made by the mysterious "Y" of Japan.

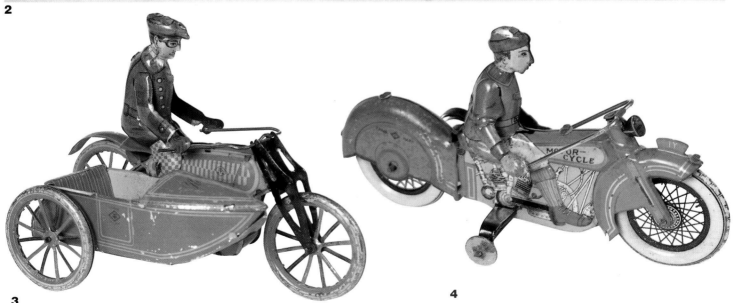

*T*hough Harley-Davidson limited its racing support after 1922, some models continued to be built, but were sold only to privateers. Few changes can be noted between this FHAC and the earlier JD. However, front forks reverted to conventional (for Harley) leading-link design similar to the road bikes, and the handlebars carry a different profile. These racers were capable of hitting nearly 100 mph on the board tracks—and had no brakes.

1925
JD

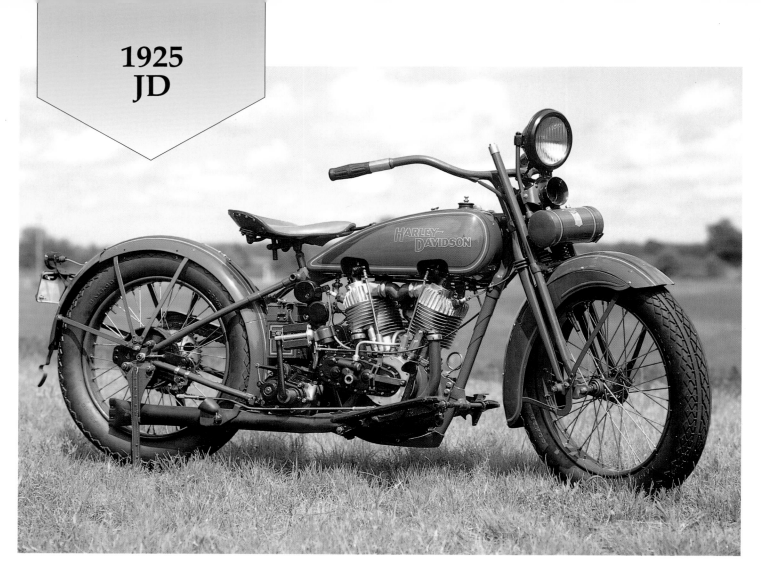

*G*reat strides were made in styling with the advent of the 1925 line. A new frame placed the saddle three inches lower than before, wider but smaller-diameter tires gave the bike a huskier look, and the fuel tank took on a rounded teardrop shape. *Opposite page, bottom row:* The smooth new tank still held both oil and fuel. A cylindrical tool box was fitted beneath the horn, but many riders complained that it rattled too much and took it off. A more comfortable bucket-style saddle replaced the old flat kind, and could be adjusted to any one of six positions.

1925
J

58

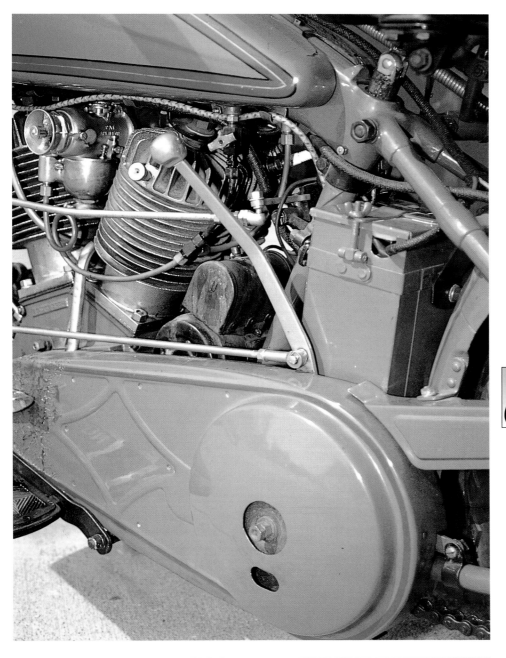

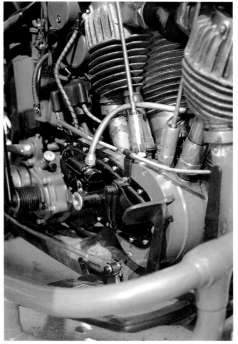

idecars were popular accessories during this period. Not only did they allow one to carry additional passengers or cargo, but they also made it safer to drive the machine in snow or slippery conditions. Passenger accommodations were more comfortable than those afforded the driver; the sidecar was suspended on leaf springs, had a nicely padded seat, and a door to ease entry. *This page, top left:* The curved silver lever beneath the seat was an auxiliary hand control for the clutch.

1

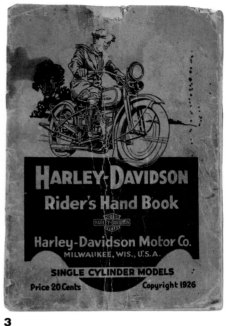

3

2

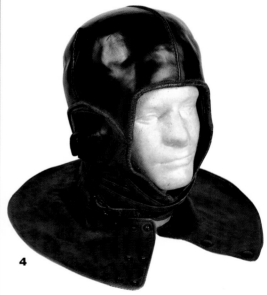

4

1923	Hinged rear fenders added for 1923 to ease tire changing; flat-twin Sport model axed	Now seen as a luxury, motorcycle sales continue to falter	Prominent styling changes are instituted for 1925: New frame lowers seat height by three inches; more streamlined fuel tank is used; wheel rims drop from 22 inches to 20; bucket saddle debuts; tubular muffler with speedster tip replaces box-style muffler
1924		Olive paint returns for 1924; box-shaped muffler used	
1925	Henry Ford drops the price of a Model T to below $300 in 1923, delivering a devastating blow to the entire motorcycle industry	Calvin Coolidge elected U.S. president	
		Walter P. Chrysler founds Chrysler Corporation	

Opposite page: 1. Featuring Harley's all-new 21-cubic-inch single, this billboard from 1926 touts the tremendous mileage that could be squeezed from every drop of fuel. 2. A 1926 single sits in the Harley-Davidson Museum in front of a photo depicting a quartet of Harley aficionados. 3. A rider's handbook from 1926 gives tips on motorcycle maintenance and safety. 4. This leather helmet was seen as the ultimate in protection during the 1920s.

1

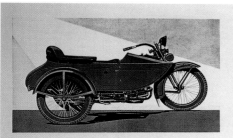

The Single Passenger Sidecar

The Double Passenger Sidecar

2

Harley-Davidson Twin 74 Model

4

Right Side View of the Single

Harley-Davidson Twin 61 Model

3

This page: 1. A 1927 factory brochure pictures the four founders along with "Six Outstanding Facts about Harley-Davidson." 2. Harley sidecars came in both one- and two-passenger versions. 3. Sales brochure for 1927 lists the price of the Model B 21-cubic-inch single at $235, while the Model J 61-cubic-inch twin went for $310. 4. Priced just $10 more than the J was the 74-cubic-inch JD V-twin—quite a performance bargain.

*T*hough economical to buy and run, Harley's 21-cubic-inch single never sold very well. Two versions of the engine were offered: a flathead with eight horsepower, and an overhead-valve variant producing twelve horsepower—an impressive 50-percent increase. Both could be fitted with electric lighting, like the flathead model shown. Ordering electric lighting brought a switch panel above the tank *(right)*, along with a generator and battery *(opposite page, top right)*. Because of its lower cost and easier maintenance, the flathead engine *(opposite page, top left)* was more popular than the ohv version.

1. High-performance Two Cam engines (still IOE configuration) had been available since 1919 but only to racers; in 1928, they were offered to the public in the 61-cid Model JH and 74-cid JDH. This 1928 Two Cam ran in the Jack Pine Enduro race. Tank graphics are from the 1936-39 era. 2. Carl Doran wore this safety gear as a board-track racer in the Twenties. 3. Wearing leather attire and a badge, this officer looks ready—and eager—to battle crime.

1926 1927 1928

21-cid singles introduced, both flathead and overhead valve versions— nicknamed Peashooters for their sound; optional colors become available (white most prominently), though this is not mentioned in sales catalogs

Gene Tunney defeats Jack Dempsey for heavyweight crown in 1926

Big Twins discard their distributor and adopt waste spark ignition for 1927

Jack Sharkey becomes heavyweight champ as Gene Tunney retires

Herbert Hoover elected to the first of two terms

GE and RCA hold the first public demonstration of television

1928 Two-Cam 61s and 74s introduced with smaller tanks and 18- vs 20-inch wheels; first front brakes appear on Big Twins

That same year, optional colors were first catalogued for $3, including Coach Green, Azure Blue, Police Blue, and maroon; cream and white cost $27; "all other colors," $24

1

1. White became an optional color starting in 1926, and by 1928, other optional colors included maroon, Coach Green, Police Blue, and Azure Blue. 2. Two Cam JDH models were quite fast for the time, and sported smaller fuel tanks and 18-inch (rather than 20-inch) wheels. 3. Harley's standard color was still Olive Green, as shown on this 1928 JD; the 1928 models were the first to be equipped with front brakes. 4. Bundled up against the cold, a Twenties rider is ready to cruise the countryside.

2

3

4

1927
JD

It's rare that a motorcycle of this vintage goes unrestored, but some that have are worth as much as a pristine example—though they don't look as nice. Once faded and weather-beaten, Harley's standard Olive Green paint took on a very militaristic look. A notable new feature on all 1927 Big Twins was the adoption of distributorless ignition, claimed by Harley to be waterproof. Both plugs fired at the same time twice as often as necessary, the "waste spark" coming during the exhaust stroke—a system Harley used for years. *Middle left:* Choke positions were engraved into the air cleaner. Keyed switches activated the ignition and lights *(bottom left)*.

THE FLATHEAD IS BORN

Launched in the late summer of 1929, the 45-cubic-inch flathead V-twin would prove to be Harley's longest-lived powerplant, still being offered in the three-wheeled Servi-Car as late as 1973. In the meantime, it would also see service in the company's military motorcycles that carried American troops during World War II, and be the basis for Harley's racing bikes that tore up dirt tracks during the late Forties and Fifties. Though larger 74- and 80-inch flatheads followed, neither would earn as sterling a reputation for reliability as the good ol' Forty-five.

Seemingly a step backwards in design, the side-valve engine had won many a customer for Indian, Harley's closest competitor. While overhead valve and even F-head (intake over exhaust) configurations were theoretically more efficient, flathead technology had advanced to the point where impressive power output was possible from an engine that remained far easier to service. With the latter being of greater necessity (and therefore of greater importance) in the 1920s than it is today, Indian was gaining ground on what had once been "the world's largest producer of motorcycles."

As it turned out, however, the flathead didn't boost sales the way Harley had hoped—though it wasn't due to any deficiencies in the motorcycle itself. The model's introduction just happened to coincide with the greatest financial disaster the United States had ever known.

Timing plays a big part in the success of any new product, and Harley's timing could not have been much worse. Just a couple of months after the flathead's debut came the infamous stock market crash of October 29, 1929; Black Tuesday. Harley's sales fell from 21,000 in 1929 to less than 4000 during the depths of the Great Depression in 1933.

As the Thirties wore on, however, the economy gradually recovered—as did Harley's sales. Shortly after the

Forty-five's introduction came a 74-cid flathead V-twin. Early Seventy-fours had their share of problems, but these were soon sorted out and the machine proved fairly reliable and sold well. A 30.50-cid flathead single debuted about the same time, becoming known as the Thirty-fifty.

As proof of the potency of the new Seventy-four V-twins, horsepower charts from 1929 bore out the fact that the flatheads slightly out-produced similar-sized F-heads, most of the advantage coming (surprisingly) at high rpms. On the road, flathead models had a bit more top end, but acceleration was about the same due to a rather sizable increase in weight.

While V-twins were the focus during this period, Harley continued to build the flathead and overhead-valve 21-cid singles (known as "Peashooters") until the Thirty-fifty flathead single came along for 1930. Though the 21 was brought back for 1932, it lasted only a couple of years. The company also introduced the first of its three-wheeled Servi-Cars in 1932, powered by the 45-cid V-twin. In an effort to further expand the scope of its business during these hard times, other variations were also tried, among them a trio of industrial engines (single, V-twin, and opposed twin), special police motorcycles, and even a special street-painter model designed to lay down the center stripes on streets. And late in 1935, an 80-cubic-inch V-twin was added to the line.

Though the flathead V-twin served the company well during this period, Harley-Davidson felt a more advanced engine would be necessary to keep it competitive in the coming years. Engineers began working on a new overhead-valve V-twin in 1931 that would prove monumental in the company's history after its introduction in 1936.

But even then, the flathead's days were not yet at an end. Harley-Davidson continued to push flathead-powered motorcycles alongside its overhead-valve offerings until the mid-Fifties, and as mentioned earlier, the Servi-Car carried a flathead through 1973. Seems many riders continued to admire the flathead's inherent simplicity, a trait that some associate with Harley-Davidson to this day.

1

1. The first of Harley's flathead V-twins came in a new size: 45 cubic inches. Referred to in company literature as the Forty-five, it was intended to compete with Indian's mid-size offerings. Because the generator was mounted vertically to the side of the front cylinder, Indian riders often derided it as the "three-cylinder Harley." 2. The instrument panel on this 1929 Seventy-four JD carries a small light to illuminate the ammeter.

2

1929

In July, 1928, Harley introduces a new 45-cid side-valve V-twin as a 1929 model; built on the same frame as the singles, it sparks enthusiasm among riders

Forty-five is equipped with a large, vertically mounted generator at the front of the engine; Indian riders nickname it the "three-cylinder Harley"

Unfortunately, the flathead V-twin arrives just as the stock market collapses on October 29, 1929, signalling the start of the Great Depression

The Harley-Davidson Enthusiast

1. Astride an older F-head Harley, the gentleman on the cover of this edition of *The Enthusiast* certainly looks resplendent in his white suit. But considering how these bikes blew oil out all over the place, it's doubtful that suit remained white for long. 2. In the early days of motorcycling, oil came in glass jars and Harley-Davidson sold its own brand. 3. This colorful oil painting depicts a rider on a 1929 Forty-five blasting up a hillside.

1. The first of the next-generation flathead V-twins was the Forty-five, which debuted as a 1929 model. 2. A 1929 factory cutaway view shows the internals of the Big Twin's leading-link "castle" forks—the last year this style was used. 3. Commercial sidecars came in a wide assortment of body styles, including this large-capacity Package Truck. The motorcycle it's attached to is a 1929 Big Twin, easily identified by its dual headlights; these were used in 1930 as well, but by then the Big Twin had switched to flatheads.

© Harley-Davidson

1

© Harley-Davidson

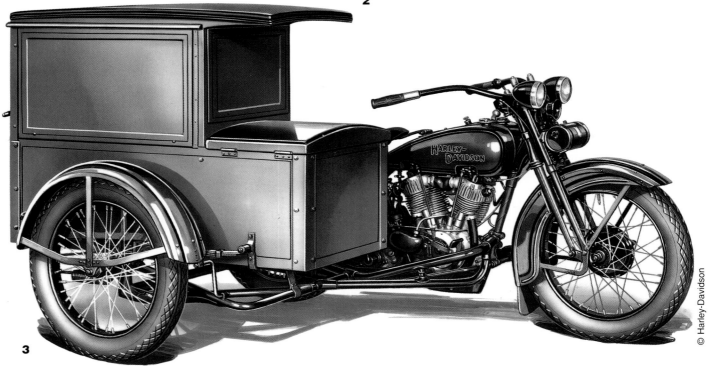

3

© Harley-Davidson

1929 1930

21-cid singles discontinued for 1929; the overhead-valve version is gone for good, but the side-valve model would later return

1929 Harleys wear dual headlights, which continue only through the 1930 model year, and some get a cylindrical tool box beneath the headlights

Thirty-fifty side-valve singles come out as late 1929 offerings

Depression cripples Harley-Davidson and the motorcycle industry in general

St. Valentines' Day Massacre thins out the Bugs Moran gang in Chicago

A 74-cubic-inch flathead V-twin is introduced for 1930, a year after the Forty-five, but suffers from early teething problems; production is temporarily halted

1. Fitted with experimental trailing-link forks, this 1930 45-cid hillclimber had special overhead-valve cylinder heads. 2. New for 1930, the Thirty-fifty single shared all its running gear with the Forty-five V-twin. 3. This 21-cid single shows off the four-tube muffler system (two tubes on each side) used on all 1929 models. These were so quiet that riders complained; in 1930, a two-tube muffler was used, mounted on the right side.

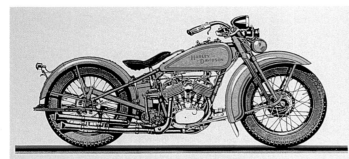

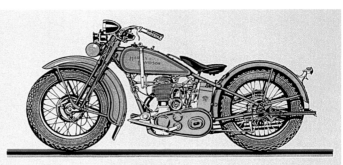

The Harley-Davidson "45" Twin

ONE of the most popular models Harley-Davidson ever built, the new "45" Twin for 1930 has a host of new features to win the enthusiastic approval of the most exacting motorcyclist. This handsome middleweight Twin is meeting with great favor among riders who demand abundant power, lightning acceleration and breath-taking speed, amazing comfort and ease of handling.

An entirely new frame design gives lower riding position, greater road clearance and more rugged strength. Drop forged forks, wider and shorter tanks, bigger tires, drop-center rims, improved clutch, enlarged front brake and theft-proof lock are a few of the more important new features on the "45" Twin for 1930.

The double front drive chain, which proved its merit

motor oiler. Like all the 1930 Harley-Davidsons, the "45" has the exclusive bullet-type headlights, spring seat post, carburetor air cleaner, waterproof lighting and ignition system and Alemite lubrication.

While the Harley-Davidson "45" is designed primarily as a solo motorcycle, it can also be used with splendid results in combination with the lighter weight "45" Sidecar, shown below. The low, graceful streamline body lends a touch of distinction to the racy lines of the motorcycle. In style and workmanship this lighter outfit is fully the equal of the "74" Twin Sidecar. Ample leg room and luggage space are provided.

Model 30D, standard 45 cubic inch Twin, $310 at factory. Model 30DL, with high compression cylinder heads, $310 at factory. Model 30DS, for use, with standard compression heads and sidecar gearing, at factory. All "45" models with Dow metal pistons. LS, Sidecar for "45" Twin, tory, without motorcycle.

The Harley-Davidson "30.50" Single

FOR anyone who desires a lighter weight motorcycle that is just as sturdily built but even easier to handle than the "74" and "45" Twins, the new "30.50" Single is an ideal mount.

Designed exclusively for solo riding, this zippy new Single has a big, rugged motor that easily turns up better than mile-a-minute speed, and develops power enough for the toughest going. The motor has moderate high compression which means long motor life and exceptional operating economy. The light Dow metal piston minimizes vibration and gives quick acceleration.

The "30.50" motor is remarkably simple and accessible. Its genuine Ricardo cylinder head is easily removable and gives quick access to the valves and piston head. Carbon can be scraped and valves ground in twenty minutes. Anyone can do the job and no special tools are required.

Except for the motor, all

parts of the "30.50" Single for 1930 are interchangeable with the "45" Twin. The new 1930 features of the "45," such as the double strength frame, drop forged forks, bigger tires, drop-center rims, wider and shorter tanks, theft-proof lock, improved clutch and enlarged front brake are standard equipment on the "30.50."

On the "30.50" Single, as on all the 1930 models, Harley-Davidson again sets the pace in electrical equipment with the new generator that automatically increases its output for night riding. When the rider switches on the headlights, the output of current from the generator is automatically increased to take care of the added consumption of current.

On pages 8 to 11 you will find complete details of design, construction and equipment of all the new 1930 models.

Model 30C, 30.50 cubic inch Single, fitted with Dow metal piston, $260 at factory.

1

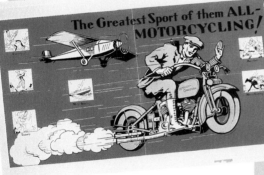

2

1. Harley's 1930 Forty-five V-twin and Thirty-fifty single carried styling similar to the big Seventy-four. 2. The sales brochure also listed prices: $260 for the single, $310 for the 45-cid V-twin. 3. Topping the line was the 74-inch V-twin, which cost $340—plus another $110 for a single sidecar, $140 for a double.

3

The "74" Twin and Sidecar

WITH this handsome, roomy, easy riding sidecar combination you can take along a passenger to share in your motorcycling fun. Deeply cushioned upholstery and two long semi-elliptic springs assure arm-chair comfort for the passenger. There is ample leg room and spacious capacity for luggage. Both are provided in generous measure.

Many important new features for 1930 make the "74" Twin the ideal motorcycle for sidecar use. It has a powerful new Ricardo head motor, a double strength frame and drop forged forks, quick detachable, interchangeable wheels and double front drive chain, to mention only a few. On the opposite page there is a full color picture showing this wonderful Twin.

For 1930 a revolutionary new feature of outstanding value—the quick detachable, interchangeable wheel—makes all three wheels of the "74" Twin and Sidecar combination

easily interchangeable. A spare wheel with an inflated tire on the rim can be carried on the rear of the sidecar. Tire changes on the road now require but a moment. Just slip out the knock-out axle, remove the wheel and put your spare wheel in place. The brake drums, bands, sprockets and chains do not come out with the wheel but remain fixed and in adjustment.

Another new feature of the "74" Twin Sidecar for 1930 is the sidecar wheel brake. This big, fully enclosed, waterproof, internal expanding brake is operated by the foot pedal simultaneously with the rear brake on the motorcycle. Together with the hand operated front wheel brake, there is now efficient braking on all three wheels.

Model 30LT Sidecar, for one passenger, $110 at factory. A two passenger sidecar, Model QT, is also available, $140 at factory. These prices do not include the motorcycle or any extra equipment such as windshield, or spare wheel carrier.

[2]

The Harley-Davidson "74" Twin

RECOGNIZED everywhere as the world's standard motorcycle, with 26 years of progress behind it, the "74" Twin today stands head and shoulders above all comers. For 1930 this famous Twin has been completely re-designed from stem to stern . . . new motor, new frame, new forks, new wheels, new tanks, new generator, everything new! For solo or sidecar riding the new "74" Twin asks no favors of anything on the road.

The new "74" Twin motor, designed along the lines of the "45" that proved such an outstanding success last season, is exceptionally accessible, clean and dependable. Its genuine Ricardo heads are scientifically designed to provide the correct turbulence of compressed gases and assure quick, complete combustion. They are easily detachable for carbon removal and valve grinding.

For 1930 the "74" frame has been strengthened at all vital points. It is now at least 100%

stronger. The saddle position is two inches lower, and the large capacity tanks are shorter and wider. Double-strength drop forged sides feature the 1930 front forks. They are built to stand the hardest service.

Quick detachable, interchangeable wheels are standard on the "74" Twin for 1930. This exclusive Harley-Davidson feature is especially valuable in combination with the sidecar. Drop-center rims and big, 4" full balloon tires complete the equipment.

Many new advancements for 1930—added to the time-tried and proved features of former models—have made the "74," more than ever, the greatest motorcycle value ever offered.

Model 30V, 74 cubic inch Twin, fitted with nickel iron pistons, $340 at factory. Model 30VL, fitted with high compression cylinder heads, $340 at factory. Model 30VS, for sidecar use, fitted with nickel iron pistons, standard compression heads and sidecar gearing, $340 at factory.

[3]

1930 1931

The Seventy-four's problems are quickly corrected and both flatheads receive critical acclaim, but few have the means to buy one

Forty-five gets a new frame with a lower seat for 1930

1930 models sport two-tube—rather than four-tube—mufflers

Harley continues to improve its products despite facing serious financial woes

A single round headlight replaces the dual-light setup for 1931, and a wedge-shaped tool box is substituted for the round one; V-twins also get a single-tube muffler

Harley adds VC commercial model, VCR road-marking model, and VS sidecar model for 1931

The Sport of a Thousand Joys!

MORE fun than flying. More fascinating than football. More thrilling than outboard motor racing. That's *motorcycling*— the sport of a thousand joys! Blood-tingling action, healthful pleasure, greater enjoyment than you ever thought possible — all are yours with a modern motorcycle. You rule the road with a twist of the throttle. Lightning get-away, speed, power in undreamed measure are yours at instant command. You go where fancy takes you. All the world is beckoning you and your Harley-Davidson to discover and explore. Get in today on this greatest of outdoor sports. Learn how easy it is to get to own a Harley-Davidson. Ask your dealer about his Savings Club and Pay-As-You-Ride Plans and let him tell you more about the wonderful 1930 models.

[1]

1. Because sidecar-equipped Harleys cost more than some cars, the company's literature stressed the entertainment value of its products. 2. On the back is a drawing of the "immense plant [that] is devoted exclusively to the manufacture of Harley-Davidson motorcycles"—complete with spewing smokestacks. 3. Harley's 1931 models could be identified by their single headlight and triangular-shaped fork-mounted tool kit.

3

ue to the financial crisis brought on by the
Great Depression, Harley-Davidson trimmed
its model offerings for 1930 from thirteen to
six in an effort to cut costs. This was the first year for the
flathead Big Twin, known as the V series. The 74-cubic-
inch engine came in high-compression (VL) and low-
compression (VS) versions, the latter intended for use
with a sidecar. *Left:* On this example, the standard dual
headlights have been replaced by a single brighter
headlight—not an uncommon practice during the era. The
battery box *(above center)* carries the company's bar-and-
shield logo. *Above right:* An ammeter was added to the
headlight and ignition switch panel.

1931
D

*H*arley-Davidson added some splashy optional graphics for 1931 in an effort to increase sales. The Model D's 45-cubic-inch V-twin came in three versions: low-compression for use with a sidecar (D), standard compression (DL), and high-compression (DLD). Early Forty-fives sported a vertically mounted generator *(right)*. *Opposite page:* The speedometer was driven off of a gearset attached to the rear wheel *(center right)*. Most owners kept the ignition and light switch keys tied together *(lower right)*.

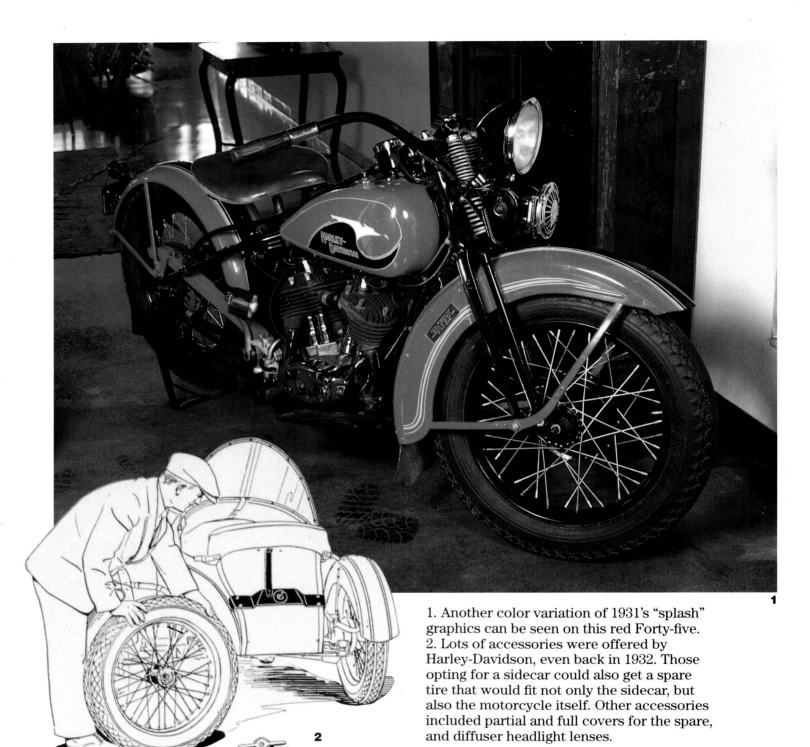

1. Another color variation of 1931's "splash" graphics can be seen on this red Forty-five.
2. Lots of accessories were offered by Harley-Davidson, even back in 1932. Those opting for a sidecar could also get a spare tire that would fit not only the sidecar, but also the motorcycle itself. Other accessories included partial and full covers for the spare, and diffuser headlight lenses.

1931 1932

Chromium plating is first offered for small parts in 1931

Al Capone is sentenced to 11 years for tax evasion

"The Ed Sullivan Show" premieres on radio

Seventy-fours gain an optional three-speed plus reverse transmission for mid-1931

Three-wheeled Servi-Car debuts in 1932 as a small delivery vehicle with the 45-cid engine; it would continue into the Seventies

Franklin D. Roosevelt is elected to the first of an unprecedented four terms as U.S. president

Amelia Earhart becomes the first woman to fly solo across the Atlantic

1. Making year-round transportation by motorcycle more comfortable were these optional windshields and leg shields. 2. Still retaining a bit of color in its brochures, Harley's news for 1932 centered around the return of a low-cost 21-cid single. 3. Sidecar prices dropped for 1932. Note that the one designed for the Forty-five didn't have its own brake, and was thus less expensive. The company's line of Package Trucks also showed reduced prices, making them more attractive as delivery vehicles. 4. Motorcycle trinkets abounded by the Thirties, when this finely engraved combination bottle opener/screwdriver was popular.

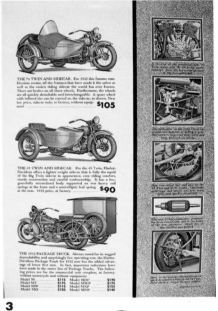

3

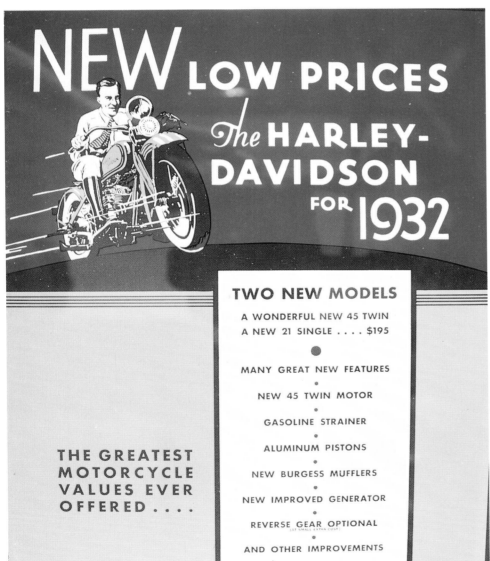

NEW LOW PRICES
The HARLEY-DAVIDSON
FOR 1932

THE GREATEST MOTORCYCLE VALUES EVER OFFERED....

TWO NEW MODELS

A WONDERFUL NEW 45 TWIN
A NEW 21 SINGLE $195

•

MANY GREAT NEW FEATURES

•

NEW 45 TWIN MOTOR

•

GASOLINE STRAINER

•

ALUMINUM PISTONS

•

NEW BURGESS MUFFLERS

•

NEW IMPROVED GENERATOR

•

REVERSE GEAR OPTIONAL
(AT SMALL EXTRA COST)

•

AND OTHER IMPROVEMENTS

2

4

1. This unrestored 1932 Model V 74-cubic-inch flathead is equipped with a number of period accessories, including wicker "trunk," brass fire extinguisher, and auxiliary headlights. **2.** Riders could keep track of their speed at night with this little add-on speedometer light. **3.** The battery box wears the original dealer's sticker—or at least a replica of it.

1932
1933

Lindbergh baby is kidnapped and found dead

1932 brings the return of the 21-cid single, but only in flat-head form

Forty-fives get a horizontally mounted generator along with a new frame and fishtail muffler, all making them look more like the Seventy-fours

Harley-Davidson builds radios for use on its police motorcycles

What would turn out to be one of Harley's most popular accessories—the Buddy Seat—makes its first appearance in 1933

1. The motorcycle depicted on the front of the 1932 accessories catalog displays a flamboyant eagle fender ornament as well as some practical features, such as saddlebags and front-wheel center stand. 2. Inside the catalog are a couple more functional accessories: a passenger pad for the optional luggage rack, and folding passenger footrests. 3. Cast-iron toys were popular during the Thirties. This one was likely hand-painted by the owner rather than the factory.

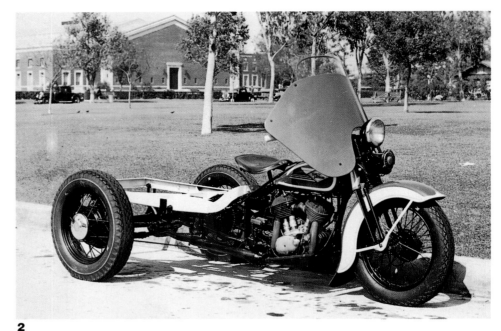

1. A booklet entitled *Let's visit the Harley-Davidson Factory* takes the reader on a tour of the expansive facilities, and shows how the machines were built. 2-4. This three-wheeled prototype wears 1934-35 graphics, and is obviously designed to carry large loads. Its intended purpose is unknown, but the large metal shield in front would suggest some military application.

1933

Olive Green dropped as the standard color in 1933; singles are offered in silver and turquoise, V-twins in a variety of color combinations

Black is now the only color for frames and forks

Adolf Hitler becomes chancellor of Germany

Prohibition is repealed

1933 would see total Harley-Davidson sales fall to less than 4000 units

1. A police officer astride his 1934 Harley-Davidson appears to be hesitant about petting a very furry dog. 2. This 1934 ad compares the punch of Harley's 74-cubic-inch "TNT" V-twin to that of boxing legend Bob Fitzsimmons—who had died in 1917. 3. Harley-Davidson offered its own oil in Regular and High-Speed grades. This five-gallon can features the new "Pour-Klean" spout.

*H*arleys boasted a new tank decal for 1934, which would be used for only two years. The featured bike is painted black with Orlando Orange insets, a no-cost option. Olive Green had been dropped after 1932 as the standard color, being replaced by more vivid two-tones. *This page, top right:* On early Harleys with foot-operated clutches, pushing down with the heel disengaged the clutch, while pushing down with the toe engaged it. *Left:* A small light illuminated the ammeter on the switch panel, and the horn face was embossed with Harley's bar-and-shield logo—an item that today is nearly impossible to find.

HARLEY-DAVIDSON
SERVI-CAR »»»»

THE PRACTICAL METHOD FOR
PROFITABLE
PICK-UP AND DELIVERY
OF AUTOMOBILES ▪▪▪▪

SAVES AN EXTRA
MAN'S TIME ▪▪▪▪

» » SAVES HIGH
CAR EXPENSE ▪▪▪▪

» » ANYONE CAN
OPERATE IT ▪▪▪▪

» » » INCREASES
SERVICE SALES ▪▪▪▪

» » » EFFECTIVE
ADVERTISING ▪▪▪▪

1. With her sailing cap at a jaunty tilt, this young lady looks like a future Harley rider. 2. This cast-iron toy from the Thirties has wheels that turn, but its rough, unpainted finish makes it look rather dowdy compared to the toys of today. The Servi-Car earned its own brochure for 1934, where it was described as being "the practical method for profitable pick-up and delivery of automobiles."

**1933
1934**

Indian and Harley agree on new racing classes that limit expenses: All entries must be showroom stock motorcycles with minimum production requirements

In an attempt to boost sales, Harley adds vivid graphics to its 1934 machines

The new look—combined with a recovering economy and a long model year— helps sales swell to over 10,000 for 1934

Bank robbers Bonnie Parker and Clyde Barrow (Bonnie and Clyde) are gunned down by police

1

2

3

HARLEY-DAVIDSON
One-Cylinder, Gasoline
POWER UNITS
Models F and G

HARLEY-DAVIDSON MOTOR COMPANY
MILWAUKEE, WIS., U.S.A.

4

1. A real Kodak moment, 1930's style. Though Harley-Davidson never claimed it to be a four-passenger vehicle, the kids on this V-twin prove that "where there's a will, there's a way." 2-4. With sales slowed by the depression, Harley looked to expand its market with industrial engines. In addition to these single-cylinder units, opposed twins and V-twins were also built.

A variety of colorful two-tones were offered for 1934, but this 74-cubic-inch VLD—along with its matching sidecar—is painted in the old Olive hue. *Opposite page:* Styling revisions for 1934 included new streamlined fenders and Airflow taillight *(left center). Lower left, this page and opposite:* A small windshield mounted on a protective tonneau shielded the sidecar passenger, and folded forward to ease entry/exit. *Above left:* The chromed rear-facing air intake came along in 1932, adding a touch of class to the bike's profile.

1

2

3

<table>
<tr>
<td>

1934
1935

</td>
<td>

Gangsters John Dillinger, "Baby Face" Nelson, and "Pretty Boy" Floyd all meet their match in separate incidences in 1934

</td>
<td>

1934 is last year for Thirty-fifty side-valve single

80-cid V-twin is offered on special order for 1935

</td>
<td>

Though the famous Knucklehead overhead-valve V-twin would debut in 1936, flathead V-twin motorcycles would continue in production into the Fifties, and the three-wheeled Servi-Car would carry flathead power until 1973

</td>
</tr>
</table>

1

2

3

4

Opposite page: 1. A sailor contemplates his dream destination, while in the background, a warbird awaits its next flight. 2. A California Highway Patrol officer makes his rounds on a 1937 Knucklehead. 3. Though the fuel tank is stamped "Patrol," it's pretty obvious this 1930s cast-iron toy was modeled after a Harley. *This page:* 1. Dale Walksler's *Wheels Through Time Museum* provided this machine to compete in the 1995 running of The Great North American Race. 2. Bearing the serial number UX3, the engine was an experimental 80-cubic-inch V-twin used as a test-bed for the recirculating oiling system introduced on all 1937 flatheads. 3. Since contestants ran day and night through all types of weather, the bike has been equipped with extra lights. 4. Though it looks much like the stock unit, this taillight is from a Crocker, another American V-twin of the era, but one built in very small volume.

THE KNUCKLEHEAD HITS

While sales of the flathead V-twins introduced in 1929 had not yet tapered off, Harley-Davidson decided to bring out a more advanced V-twin design for the mid-Thirties. State-of-the-art at that time dictated overhead valves (something Harley already had some experience with from its 21-cid "Peashooters"), so the new engine made use of this feature. Since displacement worked out to 61 cubic inches, the official name for the new V-twin was the 61 OHV. The motorcycle powered by it was called the EL.

Another step forward (at least for Harley-Davidson) was the use of a recirculating lubrication system—a real improvement, as previous models had operated on the "total loss" principal. Total loss systems had a separate tank to store fresh oil, which was gravity fed or pumped through the engine. But what oil didn't get burned off simply leaked out and was deposited on the ground—surely something today's EPA would frown upon. Recirculating systems are the type commonly in use today: Oil is stored in either the bottom of the engine (wet sump) or a separate tank (dry sump), pumped through a filter, circulated around the engine, and returned to the sump to be run through the cycle again—a much cleaner and environmentally friendly setup.

Since the EL carried its oil tank beneath the seat, the tank above the engine now held only fuel. (Previously, the overhead tank was in two parts, one being used to hold oil.) Atop the fuel tank was a new instrument panel that held the speedometer (registering to 100 mph) along with ammeter and oil-pressure gauges. This tank-mounted instrument panel would become a Harley styling trademark that's still in use today.

As introduced in 1936, the EL was an impressive motorcycle, but hardly a flawless one. While other Harleys displaced as much as 80 cubic inches, the new V-twin's more efficient valve layout allowed it to out-perform its larger side-valve stablemates—as well as most of its domestic competitors. However, oil leaks showed up early, and the frames were found to be too weak to take the added stress of a sidecar. Some of the oiling problems were fixed by midyear, while a stronger frame and further improvements to the lubrication system came for '37.

To riders and collectors alike, these original overhead-valve V-twins have come to be known as Knuckleheads. The nickname refers to the two large bolts that hold each of the right-side rocker covers in place; the bolts look like knuckles on the rocker cover "fists." Incidentally, the very first Knuckleheads had small dome-like covers in place of the bolts; the bolts were instituted as part of the midyear fix for the oil leaks that plagued the early '36 models.

With all the excitement generated by the Knucklehead, it's easy to forget Harley's other models. The 45-, 74-, and 80-cubic-inch flatheads gained styling revisions for 1937 that made them all look similar to the 61 OHV—and each other. They also got a recirculating oiling system that year, and because of all the changes, new factory codes as well: the Forty-fives were called the W series, and the big twins were now the U series. (They were formerly called the R and V series, respectively.)

Joining the 61 OHV for 1941 was a larger 74-cubic-inch version, the motorcycle it powered being called the FL. The arrival of the 74 OHV led to the demise of the 80-inch flathead U series, though the 74-cubic-inch flathead U models continued, and would be offered through 1948.

World War II prompted both a military version of the Forty-five and a special horizontally opposed flathead twin with shaft drive that was designed for desert use. The former was called the WLA, and 80,000 were built and used by U.S. troops. The latter XA model didn't fare as well; only 1000 were built, and none saw action overseas.

Despite the widespread acclaim the Knucklehead received, its life span was brief—at least by Harley-Davidson standards. It lasted only a dozen years on the market, and since World War II occurred during the midst of its reign, production wasn't all that high. But the Knucklehead formed the basis of all the big twins produced since, and today it is among the most revered of classics.

1

2

3

1936

80-cubic-inch flathead is officially cataloged for 1936, though it had been offered previously on special order

Designated the 61 OHV, later known as the Knucklehead engine, is introduced in the summer of 1936—one year behind schedule

Boasting overhead valves and more power than the flathead, the new 61-cubic-inch V-twin also has a dry-sump recirculating lubrication system instead of the old "total loss" system

New 61 OHV is offered in two models: E and EL

61 OHV engine is attached to a new four-speed transmission; it's an option on Seventy-four

and Eighty flatheads, which have a standard three-speed transmission

Tank-mounted instrument panel introduced on the E series would become a long-time Harley styling theme

1936 E-series production totals about 2000 units

Opposite page: 1. Despite the introduction of the 61 OHV engine for 1936, Harley-Davidson continued to build 45-, 74-, and 80-cubic-inch flathead V-twins. Several color combinations were offered this year, including this rather odd Nile Green and maroon. 2. Harley's brochure for 1936 didn't mention the new 61 OHV; it was apparently printed before the decision was made to announce the new model. 3. The new-for-'36 decal graced all Harley fuel tanks that year, and would be used through 1939. *This page:* 1-3. Though not very artistic, Harley's black-and-white literature for 1937 provided buyers with a lot of information. 4. Here's a good example of the over-zealous advertising often used in the Thirties. Some of the wording, such as "Lungs expand with sunkist ozone..." sounds particularly odd in today's light. 5. Although many iron toys of the period simply featured V-twin engines, this example actually has "Harley" cast into the side of its fuel tank.

PRESENTATION OF SUPERBLY ENGINEERED HARLEY-DAVIDSON

*O*ften considered the forerunner of today's V-twins, the 1936 E-series was a revolutionary motorcycle in its day. Though displacing only 61 cubic inches, the overhead-valve layout helped it produce more power than its 74- and 80-cubic-inch flathead siblings. *Top left:* Later christened the "Knucklehead" due to its rocker cover design, early '36 OHVs had smooth round "knuckles"; later in the year, these were changed to larger hexagonal nuts. This air horn was used only on the 61 OHV, and only in 1936. *Top right:* Carried over was the Airflow taillight, but most other styling features were new. A smoother teardrop tank carried the redesigned Harley decal. Another new feature was the tank-mounted instrument panel *(left)*, which remains a Harley styling element to this day.

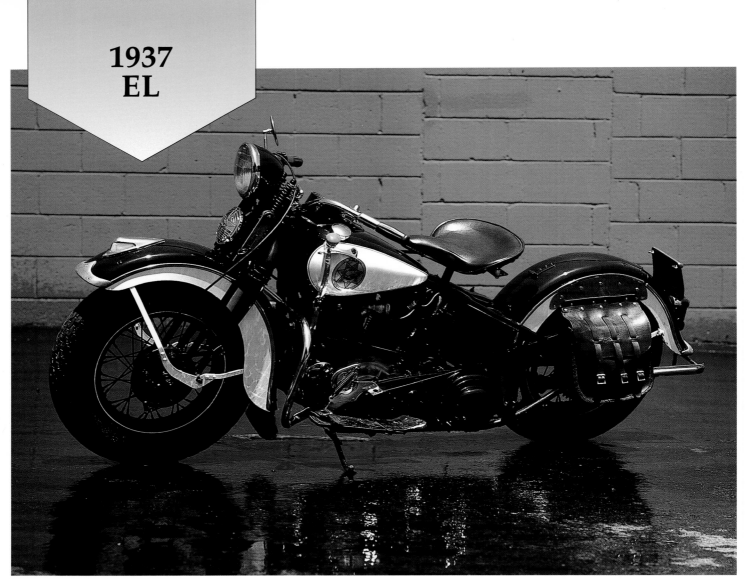

1937
EL

A few changes marked the 1937 edition of the E-series machines. This example was built for the California Highway Patrol, which had been riding Harleys since 1925. As a result, the paint (obviously) and air cleaner (less so) are not the same as on civilian models. *Opposite page:* For 1937, the speedometer *(right center)* read to 120 mph rather than 100. A front fender light *(lower left)* was a popular accessory, as were bolt-on saddlebags *(left center)*. The sprung, deeply contoured padded saddle *(lower right)* almost made up for the lack of rear suspension.

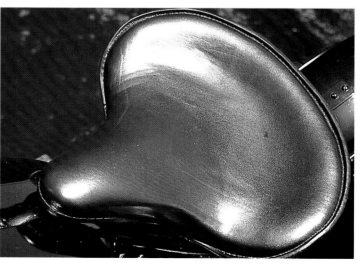

*D*espite the advent of the 61 OHV, Harley continued to offer flathead Big Twins. The former V-series became the U-series, still offered in 74- and 80-cubic-inch sizes, the latter carrying an "H" suffix. All were styled to look like the 61. *Top left:* This muffler end introduced in 1935 was used on Big Twins until 1941, and is a popular accessory today. *Top right:* Twin spot lights were a common—and useful—accessory. *Above:* Big Twin engines gained the recirculating oiling system used on the 61 OHV, and that along with the styling changes triggered the new model designations. High-compression versions of both flatheads had an "L" as the second character, so this ULH is a high compression 80-incher.

MOTORCYCLES FOR 1937

1. Since sales of new motorcycles were still slow, brochures stayed simple into the late Thirties. 2. This eight-inch wind-up toy placed junior in a precarious riding position. 3. Another wind-up toy, this one measuring 11 inches stem to stern, carries Harley lines, but the "engine" appears to be an inline three—which no company of note offered. 4. This three-wheeled cast iron Crash Car looks as though it has lived up to its billing.

1936 1937

In 1936, for the first time, groups of accessories can be factory-installed; includes front fender lamp, saddlebags, and chrome trim

Initial Knuckleheads develop some problems, most notably with top-end oiling

Douglas DC-3 aircraft begins production in 1936; it would soon put the world in the air

The first jet-powered aircraft, a Heinkel, takes flight in 1936; so does the first successful helicopter

U.S. athlete Jesse Owens wins four gold metals in the 1936 Olympics held in Berlin; Hitler leaves the stadium in disgust

Oiling problem is cured with revisions in mid-1936 and a new lubrication system for 1937; interest in the E series swells

All three side-valve models gain dry-sump recirculating lubrication systems for 1937; Forty-fives are now called W series, while Seventy-fours and Eightys become U series

1

2

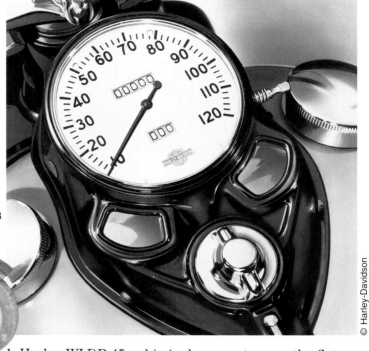

3

4

1. Harley WLDR 45-cubic-inch racers tore up the flat tracks in the late Thirties. 2. The 1936-39 tank decal had a decidedly art-deco look. 3. Though the instrument panel looked the same for 1938, warning lights replaced the previous ammeter and oil-pressure indicator. The design lasted only one year. 4. A product of Masudaya Toys, this wind-up cycle is quite detailed, though it inexplicably has a three-cylinder "engine."

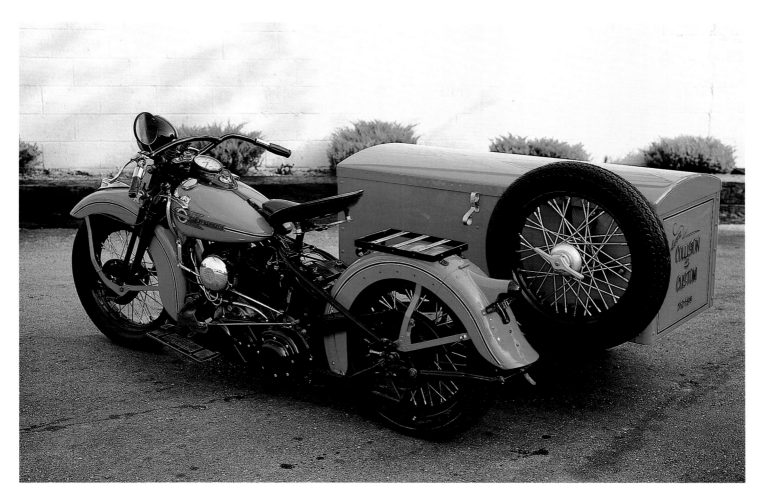

The Model U was a low-compression 74-cubic-inch V-twin designed to haul a sidecar or cargo box. Other versions of the flathead Seventy-four put out about 37-39 horsepower, but the U, with its low 5.0:1 compression ratio, managed only 32 or so. This example is equipped with a Harley-Davidson Model M Package Van, a setup similar to that used by the United States Post Office. It also has a three-speed transmission with reverse gear to make it more easily maneuverable. Note the spare tire affixed to the side of the package van; it could be used to replace any of the vehicle's three wheels.

S till a popular solo machine, the UL carried a higher (5.5:1) compression version of the 74-cubic-inch flathead V-twin. Tank and fender striping were altered for 1938, but little else changed. *Right:* Mounted below the headlight, the chromed horn was as much a styling element as a safety device. *Opposite page:* The air inlet *(right center)* was a mirror image of that used on the 61 OHV, which mounted it on the opposite side of the engine. Exhaust exited through this still-popular defuser *(lower right)*.

1938
EL

For 1938, Harley-Davidson added sheet metal covers to the top of the 61 OHV's cylinder heads, fully enclosing the valvetrain and allowing for better oil control. Though it looks stock, sharp eyes will notice that this example has received a number of chrome parts and custom touches: A large trumpet tip replaces the stock muffler deflector *(above)*; the instrument panel with its "cat's eye" indicator lamps is from a 1939 *(right)*; a custom chrome shift knob sits above 1940 tank badges *(opposite page, top left)*; chrome fender tips have been added *(top right)*; and the saddle is graced with a decorative leather skirt and a leather-and-chrome back support.

1

2

© Harley-Davidson

1937
1938

Seventy-four's bore and stroke are changed for 1937; pistons are from the 61 OHV, while the crankshaft is the same as used on the Eighty

Joe Petrali rides a modified 61 OHV to set a new American motorcycle speed record of over 136 mph in March of 1937; Fred Ham sets 24-hour record at an average of over 76 mph (including stops)

Harley-Davidson workforce votes to unionize in April of 1937; cofounder William A. Davidson dies two days after the vote

Amelia Earhart vanishes over the Pacific in 1937 during an attempt to fly around the world

Joe Louis, the "Brown Bomber," becomes heavy-weight boxing champ in 1937

The zeppelin *Hindenburg* explodes while docking in Lakehurst, New Jersey, after a transatlantic flight

61 OHV gets full valve enclosure for 1938, while warning lights replace ammeter and oil pressure gauges

1

2

Opposite page: 1. The Racine (Wisconsin) County Sheriff's Department, some of whom are straddling Harleys, stands ready for action in 1939. 2. As evidenced by the 61 OHV shown here, 1939 styling changes included tank-colored (rather than black) instrument panel with cat's eye warning lamps, new two-toned paint scheme, chrome strips rather than painted fender striping, and a new taillight.

© Harley-Davidson

3

4

5

This page: 1. Joe Petrali, famed Harley-Davidson racing star, was said to have coined the phrase "Ride a Winner" that was used on this late-Thirties dealer's sign. 2. A group of soldiers take a break from their duties to pose with a Harley-riding comrade. 3. Flathead Big Twins for 1939 mimicked the styling of the 61 OHV. Only by the distinct look of their engines was it possible to tell them apart. 4. Though it afforded little protection, a cloth riding cap would hold the rider's goggles and hair in place. 5. Looking a bit different than today's batteries, this six-volt cell was sufficient for a kick-start motorcycle. Carrying an official Harley logo, the 1940-vintage battery is a rare find.

The 1939 models received more changes than was usual during this period, most of them visual. There was a new two-toned paint scheme, tank-colored instrument panel, chrome fender strips, and redesigned taillight, all evident on the 61 OHV EL model shown here. *Left:* One mechanical change was the repositioning of Neutral to between Second and Third gears on the four-speed transmission's shift pattern; why this was done is unknown, but it was switched back to the conventional pattern (Neutral between First and Second) the following year. "Cats eye" warning lights on the instrument panel were also new for 1939.

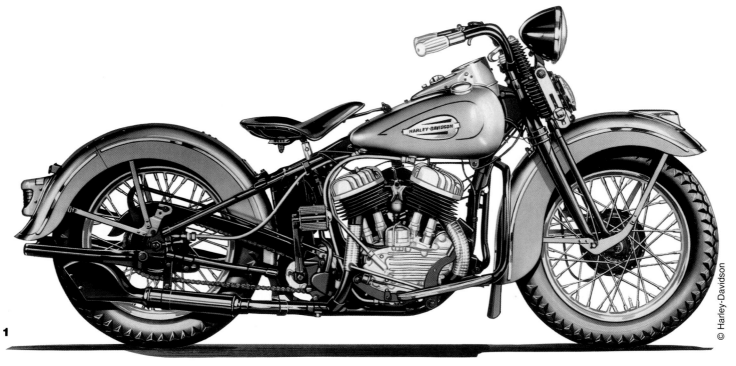

© Harley-Davidson

© Harley-Davidson

© Harley-Davidson

© Harley-Davidson

Harley's lineup for 1940 featured new tank graphics with a metal badge in place of a decal, and all models looked similar. 1. Unlike the others, Forty-fives had their drive chain on the right, and the oil tank was half of the "fuel" tank. 2. Seventy-fours—like the other Big Twins—had their oil tanks beneath the seat, a toolbox beside the rear wheel, and their drive chains on the left. 3. Eightys came standard with aluminum heads this year, which were optional on the Seventy-four. Also, an Eighty had seven cooling fins above the pushrod tubes while the Seventy-four had eight. 4. The 61 OHV could easily be distinguished by its Knucklehead engine.

1938
1939
1940

Germany invades Austria

1938 inventions: the ballpoint pen, Teflon, the first xerographic print

For 1939, "cat's eye" warning lights replace rectangular ones in a body-colored instrument panel, a new taillight is used, and Neutral is placed between Second and Third—the last being a one-year-only change

1939 Forty-five WLD Special gets aluminum heads

Germany invades Czechoslovakia and Poland; England and France declare war on Germany in 1939

New York hosts the 1939 World's Fair

Aluminum heads become standard on the Eighty for 1940, optional on the Seventy-four

All models offer 16-inch tires in place of 18-inchers

1. A happy couple riding a Harley-Davidson is depicted on this 1941 postcard. 2. Harley-Davidson built a horizontally opposed twin in 1941 for use in a prototype Jeep. Only four were assembled. 3. Major General George Grunert is shown straddling a '42 Harley XA on the July 1942 cover of *The Enthusiast*. 4. This hat is typical of the headgear worn by motorcyclists of the Forties. Each pin commemorates a special event. 5. Many riders of the period wore large gloves that not only helped quell vibrations, but also protected them from the elements—or a nasty spill.

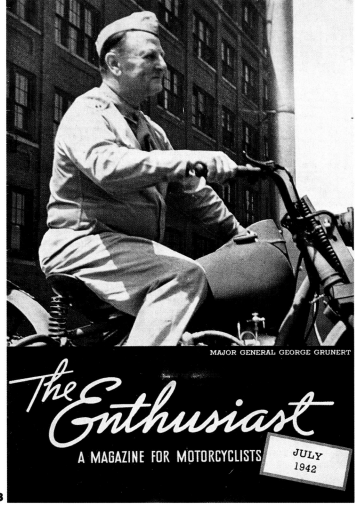

MAJOR GENERAL GEORGE GRUNERT

The Enthusiast

A MAGAZINE FOR MOTORCYCLISTS

JULY 1942

1. Harley-Davidson designed the unusual XA shaft-drive horizontally opposed twin in accordance with a military contract. Intended for use in desert conditions, only 1000 were built, and none ever saw action overseas. 2. Far more popular was the conventional WLA 45-cubic-inch V-twin, of which about 80,000 were used by American troops. This was not one of them however; it's an incredibly well-detailed model, the likes of which became popular after the war.

1940
1941
1942

1940 finds Harley building modified models for the military: a version of the Forty-five V-twin called the WLA, and a 45-cubic-inch horizontally opposed side-valve twin with shaft drive known as the XA

Germany continues its invasion of Europe

A larger 74-cubic-inch version of the Knucklehead joins the line in 1941; designated the F series, it would continue into the 1980s

Production nearly doubles between 1940 and 1941

Japan attacks Pearl Harbor on December 7, 1941, drawing the U.S. into World War II

Cofounder Walter Davidson dies in February of 1942

Automobile production ceases in February, 1942

The war prompts many developments in 1942, from tubeless tires to the first self-sustaining nuclear chain reaction

© Harley-Davidson

© Harley-Davidson

1-2. Another wartime effort was this prototype armored machine-gun outfit (note that the gun is made of wood). It appears to be based on a standard Seventy-four or Eighty flathead, complete with production tank badges. 3. The January 1943 cover of *The Enthusiast* featured Tyrone Power (left) and Preston Foster. These were just two of the numerous Hollywood actors who had already begun to embrace motorcycles.

The Enthusiast

A MAGAZINE FOR MOTORCYCLISTS

JANUARY 1943

Though rival Indian also supplied motorcycles to the U.S. military, the bulk of the machines used in battle were Harley WLAs. Wearing the requisite Olive Drab paint, these were 45-cubic-inch W-series bikes fitted with special equipment for wartime use. Early versions had the headlight above the horn; sometime in 1942, their positions were reversed. About 80,000 were built, and many were sold as surplus after the war—some for as little as $25. These surplus WLAs were often stripped down and fitted with aftermarket parts, fueling the rapidly developing customizing trend. In an effort to avoid detection during nighttime travel, military vehicles were fitted with "blackout lights" front and rear (bottom left and right) that projected only a small sliver of light.

*R*are when new—and even more so today—the XA military bike was intended for desert use and represented a vast departure from normal Harley practice. Not only did the engine boast horizontally opposed cylinders (mimicking BMWs of the day), but the XA also featured a foot-shift/hand clutch arrangement, shaft drive, and "plunger" rear suspension as used on Indians. Only 1000 were built and none were ever pressed into service, their place being taken by the Jeep. Military specifications called for a large oil bath air cleaner, shields to ward off flying sand *(right)*, and longer forks with an added shock absorber *(opposite page, lower left)*. Though the speedometer reads to 120 mph, a plaque ahead of the seat warns riders not to exceed 65 *(opposite page, lower right)*, and includes pertinent maintenance data.

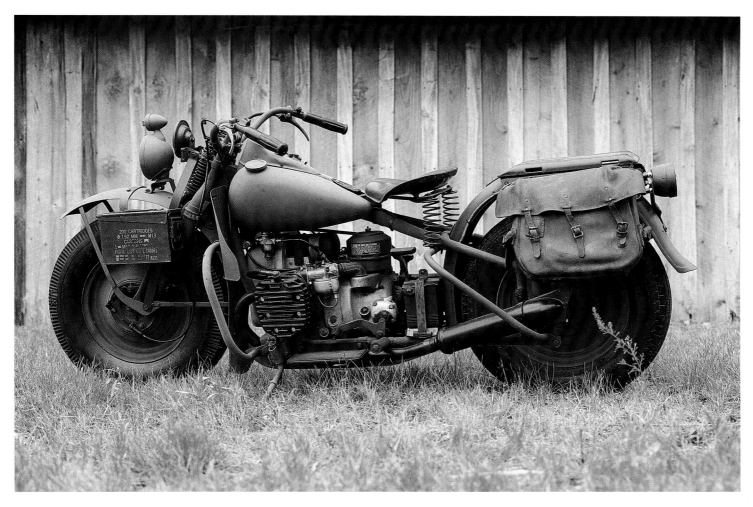

1. They may have fought on the same side, but these two servicemen chose to ride rival motorcycles off duty. That's a late-Thirties Harley Forty-five in the foreground, and a similar vintage Indian Chief in back. 2. This 1940s sales brochure points out the various models available through the local Harley-Davidson dealer, along with their features—and no small amount of patriotic rhetoric.

1943	Harley supplies 80,000 WLA V-twins to the military during the course of World War II	XA model with horizontally opposed twin and shaft drive is designed specifically for desert use, but only 1000 are built—and none see action	President Franklin D. Roosevelt dies in January, 1945; he's succeeded by Harry Truman
1944			
1945	WLA uses proven flathead engine and is dressed for battle		Germany surrenders in May of 1945
	Cofounder William S. Harley dies in September, 1943		

1

1-2. A well-preserved WLA sits in the Harley-Davidson Museum in York, Pennsylvania, in front of some wartime murals. 3. A Harley magazine ad from 1945 depicts a proud group of police officers astride their new motorcycles.

2

THE PRIDE OF BIRMINGHAM...
HARLEY-DAVIDSONS EXCLUSIVELY

CHIEF FLOYD EDDINS can well be proud of his Birmingham Motorcycle Police shown above with their sixteen new 1945 Harley-Davidson Police Motorcycles. In addition, Birmingham has five earlier models and six Harley-Davidson Servi-Cars. Like many other communities, Birmingham uses Harley-Davidsons exclusively. Their experience has proved that motorcycle equipped police officers can handle the many phases of traffic control and law enforcement work more quickly and thoroughly than by any other method.

Their experience has also proved the superior performance of fast, ruggedly built, dependable Harley-Davidson Police Motorcycles — and their ability to make police manpower more effective through covering more territory — quick concentration at scenes of trouble — and better control through closer contact with the public and constant evidence of uniformed authority. Plan now for the future of your department — built on the secure foundation of superior performance with Harley-Davidson Police Motorcycles.

HARLEY-DAVIDSON MOTOR CO., Milwaukee 1, Wisconsin

Harley-Davidsons with sidecars provide many advantages in the performance of regular and special police duties.

Harley-Davidson Motorcycles are available now for vital police needs. See your dealer.

HARLEY-DAVIDSON
Police Motorcycles

3 ★ ON AMERICA'S FRONT LINES OF ACTION ★

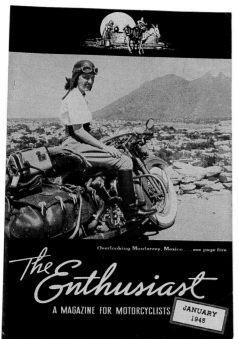

Overlooking Monterrey, Mexico . . . see page five

The Enthusiast

A MAGAZINE FOR MOTORCYCLISTS

JANUARY 1945

1

1. The woman straddling this Knucklehead on the January 1945 cover of *The Enthusiast* is the wife of one of the authors. Women riders were rare—but not unheard of—in the postwar period. 2. In the days of hand-set type, these ad mats could be dropped in place to lend an official look to a dealer's letterhead or mailings. The photo has been reversed for clarity; the mats read backwards so that the image is correct when transferred to paper. 3. Harley dealerships of the Forties carried many spare parts on factory-provided displays. These battery boxes were no doubt in better shape 50 years ago. 4. A Michigan trooper and his trusty steed in the 1940s.

2

3

4

1945 1946

First atomic bomb is dropped on Hiroshima, Japan on August 6, 1945

Second atomic bomb strikes Nagasaki, Japan, on August 9; Japan surrenders

Surplus WLAs can be purchased for as little as $25, and many get altered for street use, fueling the customizing trend

1

1. This 1946 WR racer is built on a special chrome-moly frame, and like other dirt trackers of the era, is devoid of brakes. These 45-cubic-inch V-twins were formidable machines in the hands of a skilled rider.
2. An official Harley-Davidson riding cap is festooned with various pins issued by the American Motorcycle Association.

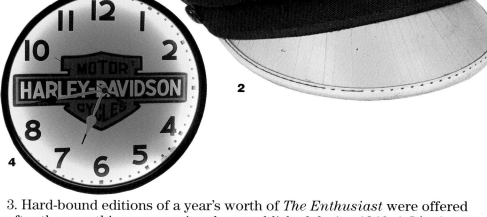

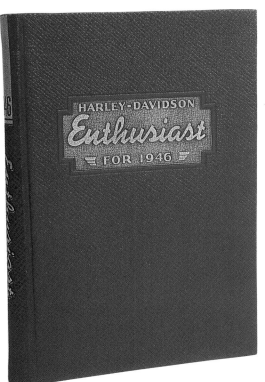

3

4

2

3. Hard-bound editions of a year's worth of *The Enthusiast* were offered after the war, this one covering those published during 1946. 4. It's always a good time to ride your Harley. This reproduction of a period clock is authentic right down to its neon backlighting.

The last of the Knuckleheads appeared for 1947 and incorporated a few changes. This is a 61-cubic-inch EL; a 74-cubic-inch version of the overhead-valve V-twin, introduced in 1941, was called the FL. A new tank emblem was used after the war *(left)*, as was a revised instrument panel *(below, right)* with Siamesed generator and oil lights. *Bottom row, left to right:* A new "tombstone" taillight debuted for 1947. Floorboards and an upright automotive-style brake pedal remained Harley signatures. Seats now held a little more padding and were deeply sculptured.

Though not the most photogenic bike around, this rare 1947 FL Servi-Car is one of only a handful ever built with shaft drive. The FL designation means that power is supplied by a 74-cubic-inch version of the Knucklehead engine, which was introduced in 1941 as an enlargement of the original 61-cubic-inch overhead-valve V-twin. The front fender is similar to those used on Harley's military motorcycles and the faded paint looks as though it might have originally been Uncle Sam's favorite—Olive Drab—but being a 1947 model, this three-wheeler would have missed World War II by a couple of years. Note the shift pattern *(lower left)* for the three-speed plus Reverse transmission.

1. In an attempt to fill the needs of soldiers returning from the war, Harley-Davidson introduced the S-125 in 1947. Built using plans acquired from DKW of Germany, the S-125 was a lightweight two-stroke motorcycle the likes of which Harley had never before offered—and which few associated with the Harley name. Advertising promoted it as an inexpensive, economical first motorcycle for young and old alike. **2.** This simple ashtray stamped with the Harley logo was a promotional gift to dealers in the Forties.

1946 1947

A new tank badge graces post-war Harley-Davidsons

Aluminum cylinder heads—which offer better cooling—are listed as a $7 option on flathead models for 1946

Harley offerings expand in 1947 to include the S-125 two-stroke single, based on a German DKW design

Jackie Robinson becomes the first African-American to sign a major league baseball contract

SAFE, MODERN
Power Riding
FOR EVERYONE
at Low Cost

JUN 2 4 1950
RICH BUDELIER
HARLEY-DAVIDSON DISTRIBUTOR
2531 SO. MAIN ST., LOS ANGELES, CALIF.

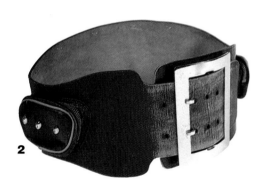

1. Harley's new S-125 certainly fulfilled the promise of "low cost," but "power riding" seems a bit of an exaggeration. 2-3. Since neither big nor small Harleys yet offered rear suspension, this kidney belt with side storage pockets was an eminently useful addition to one's riding apparel. 4. This lighted dealer sign from the 1940s has been retired from its original roost in front of Swim's Harley-Davidson in Energy, Illinois.

THE PANHEAD AGE

Even during the years of World War II, Harley-Davidson refused to rest on its laurels. While 45-cubic-inch flathead WLAs were being built in large volume for the military, engineers were kept busy improving the overhead-valve Knucklehead engine. Most of the resulting changes involved the cylinder heads, which were capped by redesigned rocker covers that looked like upside-down roasting pans. As a result, the revised engine became known as the Panhead—and with that, a new era at Harley-Davidson was begun.

While many felt the Knucklehead's life was cut unduly short, the Panhead that replaced it for 1948 offered some valuable improvements. Most notable of these was a switch to hydraulic valve lifters, which automatically took up any slack in the valvetrain and didn't need constant adjustment. As a result, Panheads produced less engine noise and required less maintenance. They also ran a little cooler, because the heads were now made of aluminum.

Just as monumental as the Panhead engine was the introduction the following year of Hydra-Glide front forks. Trading the old leading-link design (which in essence dated back to 1907) for modern hydraulically damped telescopic forks added a cleaner look while doubling front wheel travel. The '49 model was therefore christened the Hydra-Glide—an official Harley-Davidson designation, unlike "Knucklehead" and "Panhead," which were nicknames coined by riders—and that name was stamped into the upper fork covers through 1959.

The next few years brought only minor revisions, but 1952 saw the introduction of a hand-clutch/foot-shift option for the Big Twins. Like any change from tradition, this modern arrangement took a while to catch hold. But by mid-decade, most riders had made the switch, and though hand-shifts were offered by Harley through 1978, annual demand only rarely topped 200 units.

More big news came in 1953, though it affected the

motorcycle market more than the motorcycles themselves: After nearly 50 years as Harley's arch-rival, the Indian Motorcycle Company finally closed its doors. While the tendency would be to credit Indian's demise to superior products from Harley-Davidson, that wouldn't be altogether accurate. Indian had been suffering since before the war, and though competition from Harley surely didn't help matters, neither did the postwar competition from overseas. And it wasn't helping Harley-Davidson either.

After the war, both Indian and Harley-Davidson offered smaller bikes that more closely rivaled their European challengers. Indian's efforts didn't do the company much good, and Harley's had rather mixed results.

Throughout the Fifties and into the Sixties and Seventies as well, Harley supplemented its Big Twin production with smaller offerings. While the W-series eventually evolved into the famed Sportster, less impressive models also peppered the lineup—which to some, diluted Harley's image. These included diminutive road bikes, scooters, and even dirt bikes.

But back to Harley's stock-in-trade, the Big Twins. After celebrating its 50th Anniversary with some specially trimmed 1954 models (why '54 and not '53 is a mystery, especially since the 90th would later be held in 1993, not '94), Harley unleashed another milestone for 1958: the Duo-Glide. At last, the big Harleys could boast of suspension both front and rear, arriving with that innovation only about a decade or two after once-rival Indian. Unlike Indian's plunger-type setup, however, Harley used a conventional swingarm with dual spring/shock combination.

Though minor alterations were made over the next several years, a major advancement wouldn't come until the Panhead's final season. But a major advancement it was: After 60 years of having to pedal or kick their Harleys to life, riders were finally afforded the luxury of electric starting with the 1965 Electra Glide. Though that name would live on for years to come, the Panhead engine would not. It was time for a change; one that some enthusiasts felt was not necessarily for the better.

1

2

3

© Harley-Davidson

1948 1949	Panhead engine is introduced for 1948, featuring hydraulic lifters and aluminum heads	Panhead is well received, boosting sales to a record 32,000 units	Pilot Chuck Yeager breaks the sound barrier in the rocket-powered X-1 in 1948
	Four-speed transmission gets new shift pattern with first toward the rider (actually a 1947 change)	Theft-resistant steering-head lock added	1949's Hydra-Glide brings modern telescopic forks to replace the previous leading-link arrangement
	New engine is offered in two sizes: 61 and 74 cubic inches	Harry Truman remains in the White House in upset victory	Polaroid Land camera is introduced in 1949

1

2

Opposite page: 1-2. With the introduction of the Panhead engine in 1948, ads promised "fun and thrills," claiming "you can't beat riding a Harley-Davidson." 3. Save for its flathead engine, the Forty-five continued to look much like the Big Twins for 1948. *This page:* 1-3. Close on the heels of the Panhead engine came the 1949 Hydra-Glide with its telescopic front forks—and more advertising boasting of its riding comfort.
4. Kanto Toys produced this "Monkey Rider" action toy, with the monkey getting on and off the rear of the bike.

4

3

137

1948
FL

The Panhead engine introduced in 1948 brought aluminum heads for better cooling and hydraulic lifters for less maintenance. Starting in 1947, the shift pattern for the four-speed transmission was reversed, with First being closest to the rider, Fourth farthest away. Otherwise, the FL was little-changed. *Opposite page, clockwise from top left:* This example has been fitted with a nifty chrome oil filter, which wasn't standard. Tank emblems were carried over from 1947. New serrated exhaust pipes would continue into the Seventies. Tombstone taillight also returned from '47. As before, the front fender light served fashion more than function, but was a notable styling feature.

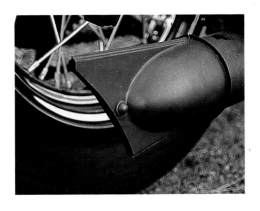

$\mathcal{S}$ince the 74- and 80-cubic-inch flatheads were dropped after 1947, the 45-cubic-inch WL was the lone flathead V-twin in Harley's 1948 lineup. It carried most of the same styling cues as the overhead-valve Panheads, so its engine was about the only thing that gave it away. WLs would be succeeded by the flathead K series which ran from 1952–56, and a 45-cubic-inch flathead would continue to power Servi-Cars until 1973.

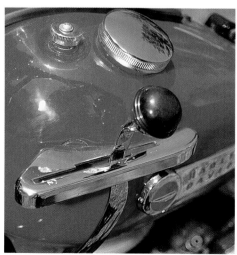

1948
S-125

To appeal to postwar buyers short of funds, Harley-Davidson built the S-125 based on a design by DKW of Germany. Powered by a simple 125-cc two-stroke single driving through a three-speed foot-shift transmission, it sported a girder front fork and rigid frame (no rear suspension). The tank bears the classic "peanut" shape and is nearly identical in appearance to those later used on the Sportster. However, without the tank badge, one would be hard pressed to identify the S-125 as a Harley. The company billed it as an excellent beginner's bike, and records show that more than 10,000 were sold in the first seven months of 1947. Surprisingly, the little bike would survive for 13 years in Harley's lineup with few changes.

*R*eplacing the famed Knucklehead engine for 1948 was the Panhead, so named because its valve covers looked like upside-down roasting pans. Beneath those covers lay aluminum heads, better at dissipating heat than the Knucklehead's cast iron. Also new were hydraulic valve lifters that ran quieter and didn't need adjustment as often as the former solid lifters, along with an improved lubrication system. Since 1941, the overhead-valve V-twin had been offered in both the original 61 cubic inches and a larger 74-cid version; that tradition was carried on with the Panhead, but not for long. This example is fitted with some popular accessories of the day: chrome crash bars, primary cover and muffler; sporty two-tone windshield; and leather seat skirt.

1948 WR

*B*uilt to compete in popular C-class dirt-track competition, the WR came out of the box in racing trim—meaning no lights, no horn, no fenders, and no brakes. The WR's 45-cubic-inch flathead V-twin was perhaps not the most powerful engine out there, but it had a broad power band that made it more flexible, a big advantage with its three-speed hand-shifted transmission. Traditional leading-link forks held up the front, while an equally traditional rigid frame was found in back. Behind the sprung saddle was a pad that allowed the rider to stretch out in a more wind-cheating posture on the straightaways without bruising his...well...more *delicate* parts.

After releasing the Panhead engine in 1948, Harley surprised its fans with the 1949 introduction of the Hydra-Glide. Named for its modern telescopic forks (replacing the age-old leading-link arrangement), it was the first time a Harley had been given a name rather than just a model designation. Attached to the new front end were handlebars that could be adjusted for position—a novel concept in the Forties. Note the fancy chrome trim on the rear fender *(this column, below)*.

© Harley-Davidson

1. Biggest change to the 1950 version of the Big Twin was the substitution of a more conventionally styled muffler to replace the former fishtail design. 2. The spirit of the wide open spaces continued to be the theme of Harley's advertising in the early 1950s. 3. Built around a chrome-moly frame, this pristine WR probably looks better than it did when it left the factory in 1950.

1950 1951 1952	Along with improvements to the basic models, Harley introduces new variations to satisfy specialized applications	The first commercially produced computer, the UNIVAC, is sold to the U.S. Bureau of Census in 1951	Richard Nixon gives his famous "Checkers" speech; General Dwight D. Eisenhower is elected U.S. president, with Nixon vice president
	Senator Joseph McCarthy makes news with his "blacklist" of "Soviet sympathizers"	The U.S. sends troops to Korea in 1951	Smaller 61-cubic-inch version of Panhead dropped after 1952
	Walter Davidson, the last of the original cofounders, dies in a car crash in 1950	1952: Salk vaccine is tested to fight polio	K-series replaces the W-series for 1952; gets redesigned 45-cid flathead V-twin with foot-shift transmission

1. A happy couple motoring through the countryside is depicted on a 1951 postcard. 2. The cover of this April 1951 edition of the *Post* shows how motorcycles were fascinating the nation's youth. 3. Even back in 1951, a host of accessories were available to enhance the beauty and functionality of a Harley. 4. "Have Fun in '51" was how Harley-Davidson hoped to lure customers into the showroom that year. Inside are illustrations showing riders escaping the big city for a trip through majestic mountains.

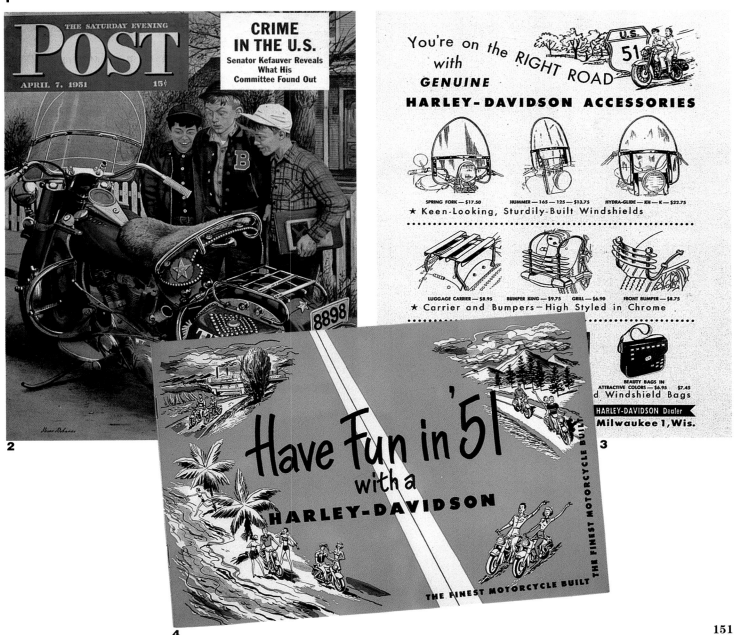

151

1951
FL Police

*H*arley Police Specials not only came with a wide assortment of equipment specific to their duties, but were often offered in colors not available on civilian bikes. Before the war they were commonly painted a special Police Blue, but many postwar models came in Police Silver. Restoration of a Police bike is made more difficult by the added equipment, accurate reproductions being hard to find. Note the fire extinguisher mounted to the rear cargo box *(opposite page, lower right)*.

1951
FL Police

ikes in decent original condition are sometimes worth nearly as much as restored examples; though they're not as pleasing to the eye, the scars earned in years of hard use give them a character not unlike that of a well-worn pair of blue jeans. Ah, the stories this old Police mount could tell.... Note the two-way radio to the left side of the rear wheel and the microphone clipped to the tank.

The big news for 1952 was the adoption of a modern foot-shift/hand-clutch arrangement for the Big Twins, though traditionalists could still get a hand-shift version—all the way into the Seventies. The Panhead engine again came in two sizes, but not for long; 1952 would see the last of the 61-cubic-inch ELs, as the 74-inch FLs garnered most of the orders. Fuel tanks were enlarged this year, and engines gained chrome-plated piston rings. Fork covers carried the Hydra-Glide logo *(center row, left)*, and would continue through 1959. The color-keyed hand grips and kick pedal were optional accessories, and are very rare today.

© Harley-Davidson

© Harley-Davidson

1. Replacing the W-series for 1952 was the K-series. These were also powered by a 45-cubic-inch flathead V-twin, but the engine was redesigned and mated to a four-speed foot-shift transmission. Telescopic front forks were fitted, and the K carried rear suspension—something other models wouldn't get for several more years. 2. The '53 Big Twins were little changed from 1952. This example is equipped with popular accessory saddlebags. 3. K-series performance wasn't great by the standards of the day, and sales never met expectations. This street-going K is displayed in front of some banners bragging about Harley's racing achievements.

1952
1953
1954

Old W-series 45-inch flathead continues to power the Servi-Car

Modern foot-shift/hand-clutch arrangement is standard on FLs for '52, though traditional hand shift is still available as an option—and will be for some time to come

1953 Big Twin speedometers numbered 1-12 rather than 10-120

Rocky Marciano becomes heavyweight boxing champ

Elvis Presley makes his first recording—for his mother's birthday

Korean War ends

Long-time rival Indian ceases production after 1953

Harley-Davidson's 50th anniversary is celebrated in 1954 with that year's models, the company apparently considering true production to have started in 1904

1-2. Harley's Golden Anniversary was promoted on the 1954 KH and 74 OHV brochures. 3. Badges commemorating Harley's 50th anniversary graced that year's models. 4. Toys were getting more sophisticated right along with the bikes they depicted. This 1950s friction model would light up its cylinders as it rolled along. 5. Miyamae of Japan brought out this nine-inch friction model during the '50s.

*F*or reasons unknown, Harley-Davidson celebrated its 50th anniversary in 1954, even though the company got its start in 1903—and would later celebrate its 90th anniversary in 1993. Besides boasting a special golden anniversary badge, the '54 models came in a variety of colors, including two-tones where the fenders were in a contrasting color to the tank. A popular dealer option was the addition of color-matched hand grips and kick-start pedal. *Right:* Speedometers now read 1 to 12 rather than 10 to 120, a practice started in 1953. *Opposite page, lower left:* The tank badge remained in script, but lost its underline.

1

2

3

1954

50th Anniversary editions of every model are produced, each trimmed with commemorative badges

1954 also sees an engine enlargement for the lightweight K model; flathead V-twin goes from 45 cubic inches to 55

The *U.S.S. Nautilus* becomes the first nuclear-powered submarine

Alan Freed describes the era's vibrant new music as "rock 'n roll" while a disc jockey in Cleveland

Elvis Presley cuts his first commercial record

The first color TV sets go on sale

American Motorcycle Association creates the Grand National Championship in 1954 to better determine the winner of the flat-track racing crown; new points system inaugurated, and Harley riders begin to dominate the leader boards

Harley-Davidson HUMMER — safe, dependable transportation that everyone can enjoy. everyone can afford and it's backed by over a half century of motorcycle manufacturing experience!

and everybody's rushing to see the Harley-Davidson
HUMMER!

specifications

Here it is . . .
the NEW
HUMMER!
famous Harley-Davidson quality
at a NEW, LOW PRICE!

Opposite page: 1. Harleys were popular on postcards in the Fifties. Here a couple enjoys a picnic lunch carried to the park in the saddlebag of their Harley. 2. The company's full-line brochure for 1956 included the entire range of cycles, as well as important technical features. 3. From the memorabilia collection of the late Malcolm Forbes comes this five-inch Japanese-made tin police bike with sidecar. *This page:* 1. Another Japanese-made tin police bike, this one an eight-inch friction model by Yonezawa. 2. Words of riding wisdom could be found in the *Rider's Hand Book*, this one supplied with a 1955 KH model. 3-4. The "new" Hummer for 1955 was little more than a renamed S-125 with a larger (165-cc) engine. 5. Another Japanese tin toy police bike from the late Malcolm Forbes's collection, this one manufactured by TYO.

New cast tank badges arrived for 1955, boasting a high degree of detail and a prominent "V" in the background, along with a similar badge for the front fender *(center right)* that even had "1955" stamped into it. Also that year, the FL was joined by a new FLH model boasting a higher-compression engine with hotter cams and polished ports—and about 10-percent more horsepower. Accessories included a handy chrome luggage rack for the rear fender *(lower right)*. *Opposite page, center right:* Standard equipment included a Jubilee air trumpet that announced your presence in no uncertain terms.

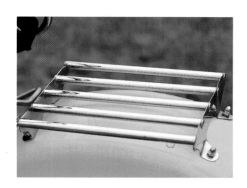

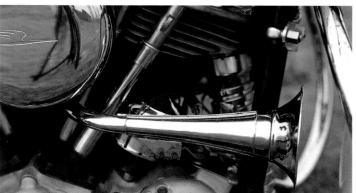

The 45-cubic-inch K series introduced in 1952 had grown to 55 cubic inches by 1954, the resulting KH models providing riders a bit more performance. In either case, a K suffix added to the model name meant the machine was equipped with lower "sport" handlebars, less chrome trim, and more performance-oriented camshafts. But the flathead-powered K was essentially a stop-gap measure until the overhead-valve Sportster was ready, which would happen for 1957; this 1956 KHK, therefore, was the last of the breed, and the last flathead motorcycle Harley would ever offer (save for the three-wheeled Servi-Car). It carries a chromed upper fork cover much like its larger FL brothers *(upper right)*. Unlike the larger FLs, however, it features a modern swing-arm rear suspension with coil-over shocks *(lower right)*.

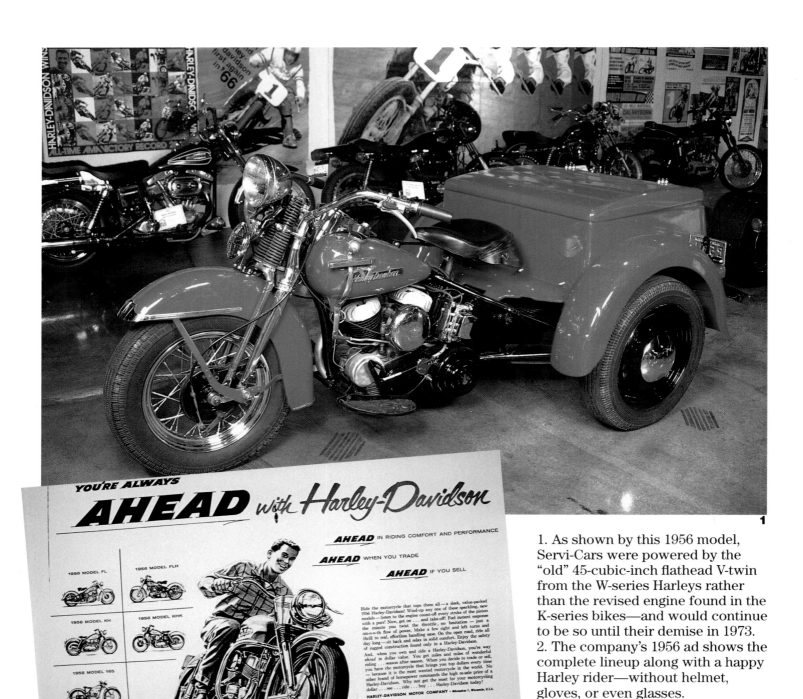

1. As shown by this 1956 model, Servi-Cars were powered by the "old" 45-cubic-inch flathead V-twin from the W-series Harleys rather than the revised engine found in the K-series bikes—and would continue to be so until their demise in 1973.
2. The company's 1956 ad shows the complete lineup along with a happy Harley rider—without helmet, gloves, or even glasses.

1955

Despite the demise of Indian, the addition of anniversary models, and Harley's greater success on the race tracks, sales don't take off.

Imports from Europe are proving tough competition, and many people are spending their disposable income on the flood of modern new appliances

Harley's attempt to cover the market with something for everyone does nothing for total sales, and the company looks ready to join Indian in failure

1955 models get new tank badges with a prominent "V" added to the script, and the classic tombstone taillight is replaced by a more conventional oval unit

Elvis' Motorcycle

1

Ready to Ride

2

3

4

1. One of a series of Elvis collector cards depicts him in an introspective moment at the helm of one of his many motorcycles. 2. Another collector card, this one catching "The King" in a lighter frame of mind. 3-4. Though it looks real, this is a highly detailed model of the 1957 Sportster made by the Franklin Mint.

1957
XL

Since the K-series was getting a lukewarm reception, Harley-Davidson introduced an updated version called the Sportster in 1957—and made an instant hit. With overhead valves topping a 55-cubic-inch V-twin, the Sportster lived up to its name, being far quicker than its predecessor. This example was painted Pepper Red over black; buyers could request the colors be reversed. *Center row, right to left:* Instrument panels held a simple speedometer, while oil pressure and generator warning lights were built into the headlight housing. "Red-eyed" valve-cover bolts were for appearances only. The engine's primary cover left no doubt as to what bike it called home.

riginally ordered and put to use by the St. Louis Police Department, this 1957 FL is fitted with the "old" hand-shift/foot-clutch arrangement, popular on patrol and escort vehicles. New round tank badges replaced the former script, but there were few other changes. *This page:* Since 1947, the hand-shift pattern for the four-speed transmission *(center right)* placed First gear back toward the rider, Fourth all the way forward; prior to that time, it was just the opposite. *Center left:* Fancy fender trim displayed a "V" theme.

n "H" suffix added to the FL designation denoted a higher-compression engine with hotter cams and polished ports bringing about five more horsepower (advertised as 58-60 versus 53-55). *Top right:* New round tank badges would last only two years—about the norm for this period in Harley's history. Nineteen fifty-seven would mark the end of an era at Harley-Davidson, as it would be the last time the Big Twin would ride on a rigid frame.

1. This well-used 1959 XR-750 racer (fitted with Daytona brakes) was found in El Salvador. 2. Only about a decade or so overdue, the big FLs could finally boast of rear suspension for 1958—as alluded to by this brochure.

The GLAD RIDE
The GLIDE RIDE
for '58

HARLEY-DAVIDSON MOTORCYCLE CO.
2801 JOHN LODGE
SO. AT GRAND RIVER
PHONE WO. 1-9576

1955
1956
1957

FLH with high-compression heads, higher-lift cams, and polished ports joins the FL in 1955, bringing with it about five more horsepower

The first McDonalds restaurant opens

James Dean is killed in a car accident in California on September 30, 1955

Dwight D. Eisenhower is elected to his second term in 1956

Sportster debuts in 1957 with 883-cc (54-cubic-inch) overhead-valve V-twin built in unit with the transmission

Tank badge changes again for 1957; now sports company name within a circle

the glad ride

Swinging-arm suspension—for *the Gladest Ride* in motorcycling. System absorbs rear wheel bounce and roughest bumps . . . sm-o-o-ths out any surface and actually *hugs* the road through the curves. Pivot point of swinging arm is supported by pre-loaded Timken bearings. Total wheel motion is 2½ inches at rear axel and is controlled by two hydraulic shock absorbers.

One ride will give you an amazing, smooth, floating sensation that will hold you spellbound . . . and, then you'll know that the unbelievable is true in the DUO-GLIDE. Try it and see for yourself!

the custom ride

Another Harley-Davidson *first* in comfort and safety . . new hydraulic rear brake that assures safe, smooth stops. Just apply pressure to the brake pedal and the master-cylinder activates the brake shoes, *instantly!* Also eliminates brake adjustments after taking-up slack in rear chain.

the glide ride

Glide Ride with Hydra-Glide . . . the hydraulically damped front fork that gives you *constant-level* riding. Fork travel is 4½ inches at front axel. Long, helical, oil-cushioned springs take up the load on rough and rugged roads. It's part of the *smooth-ride pleasure,* packed into the new 1958 DUO-GLIDE.

the power ride

74 cubic inches of smooth, *"two-fisted,"* OHV dynamite are nested snugly in the DUO-GLIDE frame. Available in FL or FLH series, the DUO-GLIDE engine features new, large-finned aluminum heads, hydraulic valve lifters, hemispherical combustion chambers and *tremendous* power to put you out front and *keep* you there.

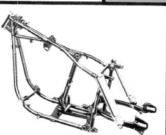

the dream ride

Up front, hydraulic forks . . . in back, swinging-arm suspension . . . and mid-way, the sensational *spring-loaded seat post*—a triple treat in riding comfort. All alone or riding double, the DUO-GLIDE seat post *springs* into action, keeping you on an *even keel* at all times. Another DUO-GLIDE *extra!*

the quality ride

The DUO-GLIDE frame is a *symbol* of strength . . . a steel structure of *finest craftsmanship* designed to stand up under *all* conditions. Made from seamless steel tubing, the frame is all-steel welded for maximum strength.

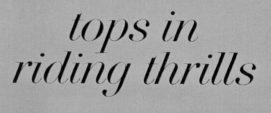

tops in riding thrills

1

1. Inside the 1958 brochure was an explanation of the various components that contributed to the Duo-Glide's "riding thrills." In addition to the Hydra-Glide forks and new swingarm rear suspension, the Duo-Glide still carried a spring-loaded seat post, the combination that claimed to provide "a triple treat in riding comfort." Also new was a hydraulically activated rear brake.
2. I.Y. Metal Toys produced this friction model complete with passenger—and Saturn gas-tank logo, which defies explanation.

2

After an impressive debut season, the XL received a horsepower boost for 1958 via increased compression and larger valves. Appearances changed little. Just like Harleys of old, the XL's instrument panel *(bottom left)* carried dual keyed switches for ignition and lights, but they now included flip-away weatherproof covers. *Bottom right:* Unlike the Big Twins, the Sportster's foot shift was on the right side, following the British format—odd, because moving up to an FL required the rider to learn a new technique.

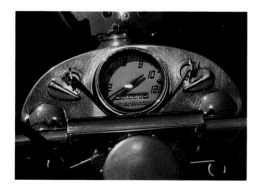

*F*inally, after decades of having to rely on only a sprung saddle for "rear" suspension, the 1958 Big Twins were given a modern swing-arm suspension in back. High-speed stability problems showed up early, but were quickly traced to a fault in the steering head and fixed. Two versions continued to be offered: The milder, low-compression FL engine ran cooler than the hopped-up FLH, making it better suited to around-town driving. *Lower left:* Note the prominent rear grab bar, a common period accessory before the advent of backrests.

*H*arley's Big Twin was popular with both the public and municipalities, many in the latter category being used for police duty—but not all. This 1959 FL was pressed into service as a funeral escort, and therefore missed out on all the excitement enjoyed by its police-ridden siblings. It had nothing to be ashamed of, however, being dressed with many of the same accessories—siren, red lights, and radio—as the pursuit models.

*I*ntroduced in 1959 as a performance-oriented on/off-road version of the Sportster, the XLCH was lighter than its XLH sibling, and featured a magneto-generator *(top right)* along with high exhaust pipes, solo seat, smaller "peanut" tank, and semi-knobby tires. It also featured the now-famous "eyebrow" headlight nacelle, still a Sportster trademark. Both versions got a slight horsepower boost through redesigned cams.

1

2

1957 **1958** **1959**	Sportster proves to be an instant hit, providing much-needed revenue Russia successfully launches the first space satellite, Sputnik I, in 1957; a U.S. satellite, Viking, blows up during launch	Both Russia and the U.S. test intercontinental ballistic missiles Big FL model finally adopts rear suspension in 1958, becoming the Duo-Glide Neutral indicator light is added to Big Twin in '59	Performance-oriented Sportster XLCH introduced in 1959 New arrow tank badge debuts Sportster XLH gets large headlight nacelle

1

Opposite page: 1. The 1960 XLCH showed little in the way of change. Though it was never officially addressed, some insist that CH stood for "Competition Hot." 2. The standard XLH was a bit tamer and aimed more at highway use with its larger tank and full-coverage fenders. The large headlight nacelle came on in '59. *This page:* 1. For 1961, Harley-Davidson joined up with Italian partner Aermacchi to produce the Sprint, a 250-cc horizontal single. Shown here inspecting the first Sprint shipped to the U.S. are (left to right) William Harley, William Davidson, and Walter C. Davidson, heirs of the original founders. 2. The "arrowhead" badge introduced on the FLs for 1959 was carried on for 1960. 3. Offered between 1961 and 1974, Sprints were available in various guises from street bikes to racers in both 250- and 350-cc versions.

2

3

1960
FLHF

*H*arley FLs entered the Sixties with a large headlight nacelle similar to that used on the previous year's Sportster. The FLHF designation means this FL boasts the *H*igh-performance engine and *F*oot shift, though the last is not identified on the oil-tank decal *(opposite page, top right)*. Tank badges changed again this year, now featuring an arrowhead theme. Our featured bike wears the popular "2-into-2" crossover exhaust system, which was optional.

1-2. The 1962 Duo-Glide *(above)* differed little from the 1961 version *(right)*, though a different striping pattern was used. Both wore a re-designed tank badge boasting a new star theme. 3. The Sportster XLH didn't change much in the early '60s aside from getting new tank badges every couple of years.

1959
1960
1961

More and more Harley owners are building personalized machines as custom accessories abound

Rock 'n roll loses three of its brightest stars in a 1959 plane crash: Buddy Holly, Ritchie Valens, and the Big Bopper

Topper scooter is introduced in 1960 but would last only two years; biggest promotion comes from "Kookie" on TV's *77 Sunset Strip*.

FLs get a large headlight nacelle like the XLH for 1960

U.S. U-2 spy plane is shot down over Russia

John F. Kennedy barely defeats Richard Nixon for the U.S. presidency in 1960

The laser is invented

FLs get a "star" tank badge for 1961

Italian-built Sprint imported for 1961 has a 250-cc four-stroke horizontal single engine

1

2

3

1. The KR-750 remained a popular choice of racers in the 1960s—despite its antiquated flathead V-twin engine. This 1962 model was raced at tracks throughout central Illinois. 2-3. Harley's Topper motor scooter was promoted in 1962 with this splashy brochure. Inside was a description of its primary features. 4. Here's another example of a lighted friction-drive Japanese tin toy, this one depicting a policeman on his mount.

4

1

2

1961 **1962** **1963**	First the Russians and then the Americans send men into space	1962: John Glenn becomes the first American to orbit the earth	A new "diamond" tank badge debuts in 1963
	The Bay of Pigs assault on Cuba fails	The Cuban Missile Crisis takes place in 1962: U.S. blockades Cuban ports and convinces Russia to dismantle nuclear missiles sent to Cuba	The Beatles release their first U.S. hit, "I Want to Hold Your Hand"
	U.S. servicemen are sent to Vietnam in 1961—as advisors		President John F. Kennedy is assassinated in Houston on November 22, 1963; Lyndon Johnson takes over as president
	Harley-Davidson golf carts debut, and would continue to be popular for many years		

1

Opposite page: 1. The Sportster XLCH got new tank graphics and a larger seat for 1961.
2. Though the tank badge was about the only part of the Sprint that looked familiar to Harley aficionados, the Italian-built single sold fairly well. *This page:* 1. Harley's full lineup of 1962 models can be seen in this factory promotional photo. 2. The "H" version of the Sprint was introduced in 1962 featuring bobbed fenders at both ends, semi-knobby tires, and a high-mounted exhaust. 3. The Pacer was one of three 175-cc two-stroke singles introduced by Harley-Davidson for 1962. It was intended for street use. 4. The Scat was an on/off-road version of the Pacer. A third variant called the Ranger was a trail bike (without lights). None offered rear suspension until 1963, by which time the Ranger was already gone. The Bobcat, with a sporty one-piece body, was brought in for 1966, which would prove to be the final year for these little singles.

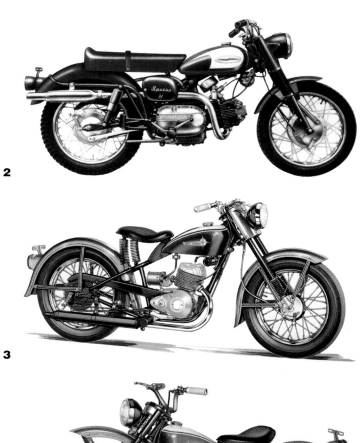

2

3

4

ince its debut in 1958, the Duo-Glide had become a big favorite among riders and dealers alike. Power and dependability had been improving each year, and there was an ever-growing assortment of custom accessories from which to choose. Chrome-plated pieces were particularly popular, and this FL boasts a host of brightwork, from the front fender trim to the fishtail muffler. Even the shock covers, toolbox, and oil filter have been treated to a chromium bath.

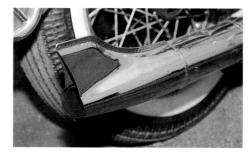

1963
Topper

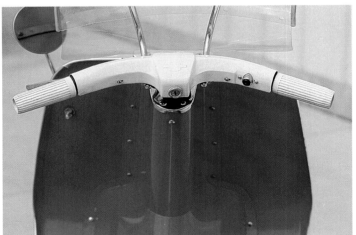

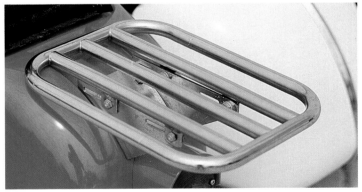

*T*o capitalize on the scooter craze then afflicting the country, Harley brought out the Topper scooter in 1960. Its 165-cc two-stroke horizontal-single engine was started with a hand-operated recoil starter (like a lawn mower) and drove through a variable-ratio transmission (like a snowmobile) known as "Scootaway Drive." Up front was a simple leading-link fork *(opposite page, bottom right)*. Beneath the seat was a cargo box and many owners also added a luggage carrier. Though the combination must have proved interminably slow, one could even affix a sidecar to the rig, providing (at least in theory) seating for up to three people.

it's fun ..... ride one!

DIAMOND MATCH DIV. ➔ NEW YORK, N.Y.

1

2

1. A late-Fifties Harley matchbook advertisement carries a rather unimaginative tag line. Slogans would get a little better as the years progressed. 2. Making the scene in 1964, "Davey" was one of the "Weird-Ohs" created by Big Daddy Roth, customizer of both cars and cycles. 3. Harley's back-to-back wins at Daytona in 1962 and '63 helped to boost the company's performance image.

HARLEY-DAVIDSON

again sweeps Daytona Beach

200-MILE NATIONAL CHAMPIONSHIP

Number One Rider on Number One Brand Again Wins America's Number One Race Meet

For the second year in a row Roger Reiman, Kewanee, Illinois, No. 1 rider, mounted on a Harley-Davidson, beat all comers in the 200 mile Daytona Road Race in a driving rain storm. On the straightaway Reiman's speed topped 130 mph; Reiman's average speed was 90.04 mph.

Mert Lawwill, San Francisco, California, came in second for a one/two win in the 200 mile classic. Lawwill, Harley-Davidson mounted, steamed through the driving rain for second place, 40 seconds behind Reiman.

In the amateur event, rider Wayne Cook, Harley-Davidson mounted, bested the entire field and set a *new record* with an average speed of 92.43 mph.

Another year of racing opens with a sweeping victory by Harley-Davidson at Daytona.

Roger Reiman

Wayne Cook

Mert Lawwill

MAY, 1965

3

1-3. In a fit of expansion, Harley-Davidson ventured into golf carts in the early Sixties, offering both gasoline and electric models. Gas versions used a two-stroke engine coupled to a variable-ratio transmission. An engine-mounted generator also served as an electric starter. Simple and cost-effective, this system worked well and is still used today. Not surprisingly, golf cart accessories were plentiful. 4. This 12-inch tin toy is battery operated, and has a working headlight along with a rider that mounts and dismounts when the switch is thrown.

hough the Duo-Glide had changed little since its introduction in 1958, owners were never at a loss for accessories to make their pride and joy look different from the rest. *Top row:* Chrome accoutrements abound on this example, including engine and floorboard guards, instrument-panel trim rail, and front fender rail.

1964
XLCH

Entry-level and performance-oriented riders alike could find an attractive mount in the Sportster series. While the XLH was aimed at the touring set, the lightweight XLCH appealed as a sporting entry. Yet despite its sporting aspirations, the only gauge provided was a speedometer *(right)*. *Opposite page:* Aside from its V-twin engine *(upper left)*, which looked a lot like the upcoming Shovelhead Big Twin, the Sportster shared few styling elements with the FL though tank badges *(right center)* were the same.

**1965
FL**

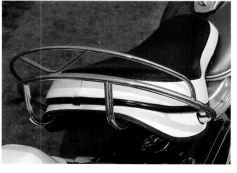

*N*ineteen sixty-five saw the introduction of the electric starter at Harley-Davidson, as well as the last of the venerable Panhead engines. With the addition of an "electric leg," the Duo-Glide became known as the Electra Glide, opening a whole new era for the company. Harley legend was rife with stories of riders being nearly launched over the handlebars while trying to start a recalcitrant engine (some accounts even had riders coming away with broken legs), so the addition of an electric starter on the FLs made them more attractive as touring mounts.

THE SHOVELHEAD DIGS IN

The Panhead had just reached its pinnacle in 1965 with the addition of electric starting when Harley-Davidson replaced it with a revised engine boasting (you guessed it) new heads. Called the Shovelhead due to its inverted scoop-shaped valve covers, the engine could now breathe deeper than before, resulting in a 10-percent increase in rated horsepower.

To the casual observer, the new Shovelhead looked much like the Sportster's engine, which was already ten years old by that time. However, the Sportster engine was built in unit with its transmission, whereas the Big Twin, as always, was a separate entity. And though the Shovelhead has since elicited strong feelings among many riders—some positive, some not—the two decades that the Shovelhead powered Big Twins were perhaps more noteworthy for the changes that occurred in the company than for any changes to the V-twin engine itself.

After going public with its stock in 1965, Harley-Davidson found itself the target of several takeover bids. One of them eventually materialized in the form of a merger with sporting-goods manufacturer American Machine and Foundry (AMF) at the beginning of 1969.

AMF poured money into Harley-Davidson in an effort to expand production, but the conglomerate also stepped in to help dictate policy. This didn't always set well with some long-time Harley managers, and though production did indeed increase, quality tended to go in the opposite direction. It was also during these years that Harley's model line was expanded with a host of small, imported motorcycles—few of which lasted very long and none of which did Harley's image any good.

Of course, hindsight provides a far clearer view than foresight, and the decision to broaden the company's product line by adding smaller, cheaper machines may have been a perfectly logical one at the time. The problem

Harley-Davidson faced, however, was the same one that plagued U.S. automakers: The Japanese were far ahead on this score, and it was proving increasingly difficult to beat them at their own game.

Furthermore, Harley's traditional offerings were also being threatened. For a decade after its release, the Sportster was the almost undisputed "King of the drags." By the late Sixties, however, some of the larger British bikes were nipping at its heels, and then Honda really upset the apple cart with its revolutionary 750 Four.

As Harley-Davidson soldiered on through the decade, it became increasingly apparent that hard times lay ahead unless some changes were made. After dumping charges filed against the Japanese manufacturers in April of 1978 proved futile, a handful of Harley executives approached AMF with a plan: In what would later become a rallying cry from owners, dealers, and employees alike, they offered to *buy back* the company.

With profits sluggish and the proposal inviting, AMF agreed to the offer, and in June of 1981, Harley-Davidson was on its own once again. A revived spirit of pride seemed to spread throughout the faithful, and the company's position—and products—slowly improved. The FXR, with its five-speed transmission and isolated drivetrain, added a more modern entry to the line late in 1981, while the next two years brought some interesting Sportster models that brought new riders into the fold.

This isn't to say, however, that Harley-Davidson sat on its hands during the AMF years. Indeed, one of the company's most influential products was born under AMF's auspices: the FX Super Glide, the industry's first factory custom.

Introduced in 1971, the Super Glide was not an overwhelming success at first, but it spawned a host of subsequent customs that eventually became Harley's stock in trade. However, perhaps the greatest achievement of the AMF years wouldn't be forthcoming until well after the buy-back program had returned the company to private ownership.

1

2

1. According to Harley-Davidson, hotter cams and a new carburetor resulted in a 15-percent increase in horsepower for the Sportster in 1966. 2. For '67, Harley boasted of the Sportster's feats on the Bonneville salt flats, though these were with highly modified machines. Nevertheless, the company claimed that "Nobody builds a faster stock motorcycle." 3. It's rare nowadays to find a Sixties FLH this close to stock condition. There are a few chromed accessories on this '68, but it's otherwise original.

3

1966 1967

Shovelhead engine is introduced for 1966; brings a 10-percent increase in power via better breathing

Though more powerful, Shovelhead does not spur sales as did the Panhead

Harley continues to sell the 250-cc horizontal four-stroke Sprint single, built by Aermacchi of Italy

The partnership with Aermacchi also brings a variety of tiny 50- to 90-cc motorbikes starting in 1965 and running into the Seventies

Heavyweight champion Cassius Clay changes his name to Muhammad Ali in 1966

Three Astronauts, Roger Chaffee, Virgil Grissom, and Edward White, are killed during a test launch of Apollo 1 in 1967; the first fatalities of the space program

First successful heart transplant is performed in South Africa by Dr. Christiaan Barnard in 1967

New 125 cc!
Over 70 mph!
Under 175 lbs!
Over 70 mpg!
Under $400!

No matter how you put the numbers together, Rapido stacks up great. This is the new one from Harley-Davidson with a power-to-weight ratio that combines miles per hour with miles per gallon all day long. Rapido's quick acceleration and effortless top speed will startle you. The fine balance, big brakes and sure suspension will reassure you. So will the price tag. Dollar for dollar, there's nothing like Rapido on the road. Or on the track. Ride it. Compare it. Find out what plus-engineering is all about. Let Harley-Davidson put some fun ahead of you. Rapido 125. At the Harley-Davidson dealer near you.

Harley-Davidson
priced to meet competition.
+ engineered to beat it.

Prices F.O.B. Warehouse

IT'S
LEVY-GARDNER-LAVEN presents
ELVIS in "CLAMBAKE"
TECHNISCOPE® TECHNICOLOR®

1. Built to attack the banks of the Daytona race track, this 1968 KR with its flathead engine managed to qualify for the prestigious 200-mile event, but didn't win. 2. The Rapido, introduced in 1968, was one of Harley's more successful imported offerings; it was sold through 1977. 3. Elvis Presley rode a full-dresser in the 1967 release of *Clambake*.

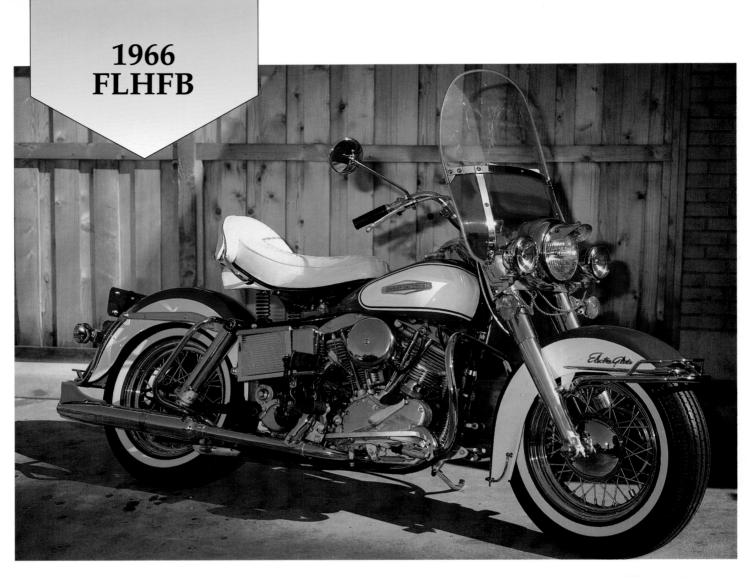

eplacing the venerable Panhead engine for 1966 was the Shovelhead, which profited from better breathing and a new carburetor to produce about five more horsepower—something the big FLs could use now that they were so frequently ladened with touring gear. Appearance changed little overall, though a revised paint scheme and redesigned tank badge arrived with the new engine.

S till powered by the 45-cubic-inch flathead V-twin introduced in 1952, the KR was capable of winning races well into the Sixties. Specifications of the flathead would seem to leave it hopelessly ill-equipped for competition, but the KR defied the odds, and experienced riders continued to end up in the winner's circle until the British machines eventually conquered the dirt tracks in the late Sixties. Tanks were of the "peanut" variety and carried the current Harley badge. *Opposite page, center right:* the "R" on the oil tank signified a racing model. This KR is set up for the dirt tracks; road-race versions came equipped with rear suspension, thinner tires, and a larger fuel tank.

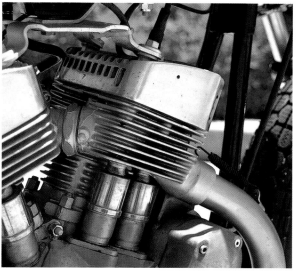

1966
Sprint

*I*ntroduced in 1961 as a result of a cooperative venture between Harley-Davidson and Aermacchi of Italy, the Sprint boasted a 250-cc horizontal four-stroke single and was quite popular at first. Little had changed by 1966, though styling had become more modern, and by that time, both street and on/off-road (Scrambler) versions were offered. For 1969 the engine was enlarged to 350 ccs on the street-going Sprint—now called the SS—while the Scrambler didn't get the larger engine until 1972. Both models disappeared after 1974, to be replaced by two-stroke machines. *Right center:* Though the crankcase said Harley-Davidson, the engine was built by Aermacchi.

1967
XLH

or 1967, Sportsters gained the electric starter introduced on Big Twins two years earlier—at least the XLH version did. The sportier XLCH kept its kick starter, which remained on the XLH as a backup to the electric leg. As before, the XLH carried fancier trim, including a large polished headlight bezel, chromed rear shock covers, a larger fuel tank, an instrument panel mounted just above the tank *(right)*, and a two-person seat. Despite its luxuries, however, the XLH was outsold by its sportier counterpart in '67.

1

the Harley-Davidson out-performers
...out-perform everything on two wheels!

THE TWO BIG STORES

HARLEY-DAVIDSON IN LOS ANGELES
2531 South Main St.
Los Angeles, Calif. 90007
Phone 749-6235

OR

SAN FERNANDO VALLEY
HARLEY-DAVIDSON
16113 Sherman Way
Van Nuys, Calif. 91406
Phone 780-9864

ELECTRA GLIDE. 1200 cc's of finely-tuned power ready to respond. Freeway speeds. City traffic. Rough country roads. Only one motorcycle lets you handle them all — all day long. The care that goes into building this machine is evident in every ride. It is the ultimate in two wheel motoring.

SPORTSTER. They all talk about this 900 cc cycle and then line up behind it. It is the fastest street bike in the world. And every component measures up to that speed. The two models, CH and H, let you choose between electric and kick starting. Ride either one just once and there's no other choice.

SPRINT. After capturing every honor at 250 cc, the new Sprint now moves up with a headstrong 350 cc engine. To match that power, there's a new carb, new dry clutch and new mufflers and pipes. This one just won't quit. Available as a swinging street scrambler, SS, or as a pure scrambling machine, ERS.

RAPIDO. 125 cc's of heady excitement on a lightweight frame. Lots of wheelies and low end torque. The new MLS is a hot scrambler with high pipe, large sprocket and special rear tire. Off the road, it runs like a rabbit hound. The ML street model does the same thing on pavement. Both are great blends of motorcycle performance and economy.

M65. The gold dust twins — M65 and M65 Sport. They give you zip-around-town convenience at a miles-per-gallon figure that makes walking seem expensive. And with the name Harley-Davidson on the tank, you get engineering excellence as standard equipment. You also get good dealer service, financing and established resale value. A lot for under $235.

APR 2 6 1969

2

1-2. The "out-performers" was how Harley chose to describe its 1969 model line, stating that the Sportster was "the fastest street bike in the world." That claim faded with the introduction of the Honda 750 later in the year. The brochure also stated that the economy of the little M65 two-stroke was such that it "makes walking seem expensive."
3. *Hell's Angels '69* was one of the many little-known biker movies that came out in the Sixties.

3

1968 1969

125-cc Rapido two-stroke single joins the line in 1968, and would continue through 1977

1968: Martin Luther King, Jr. is assassinated in Memphis, Tennessee, in April; presidential candidate Robert Kennedy is assassinated in California in June

Lyndon Johnson refuses to run for a second term; Richard Nixon is elected U.S. president

Harley-Davidson begins attracting attention from potential buyers

Harley-Davidson merges with sporting-goods manufacturer American Machine and Foundry Company (AMF) in January of 1969

AMF offers an injection of cash and more manufacturing facilities

1

2

1-2. In the late Sixties, Harleys were still King of the Drags. This stripped racer started out as a 1969 Sportster, and after being competitive for several years, was retired as an aging relic. It has since been restored—and upgraded—and is now back in action, running faster than ever. Solid chrome rods replace the shocks in back, resulting in a hardtail frame.

*T*he CR250 was an offshoot of the Aermacchi-built Sprint, and was designed with flat-track racing in mind. Stripped of non-essential hardware like brakes, lights, and fenders, the CR was truly a race-ready machine, sporting a rigid rear frame and weighing in at just over 200 pounds. Still displacing 250 ccs, the little four-stroke single gained revised carburetion, higher compression, and free-flowing exhaust, all of which made it a competitive mount right out of the box.

1968 XLCH

portsters ruled the road in the Sixties, and this '68 XLCH represents the elemental form of the breed. Being a CH (which some felt stood for "Competition Hot") it carries a kick starter and small "peanut" tank, and this example is fitted with a sprung solo saddle. Adding to its sporting appeal are low handlebars and a matte-black covering on top of the fuel tank, which wore the "corporate" badge shared by all Harleys that year.

At the opposite end of the Sportster spectrum lies this 1968 XLH, laden with virtually every extra offered by the factory. *Right:* A custom windshield with carrying pouch fits snugly around the square-shouldered headlight bezel, which mounts turn signals at its lower corners. Other extras include chrome fender tips, chrome crash bar, padded backrest, and hard-shell saddlebags. The standard electric starter resides just behind the rear cylinder.

1969
XLCH
Chopper

o few early stock Sportsters remain today because many found themselves the basis for that icon of Seventies motorcycling, the chopper. In the case of this 1969 XLCH, little remains of the original bike but the engine, and even that has been given much attention. The custom hardtail frame is supported by long "springer" forks up front, and carries a custom fuel tank along with a special octagonal chrome oil tank beneath its thinly padded seat. The tall "sissy bar" with Iron Cross taillight were *de rigueur* for the era. *Opposite page, bottom left:* Note that the shift lever has been relocated to the frame's front downtube to allow shifting while the rider's foot is on the highway peg. Truly a rolling work of art, choppers such as this are difficult to ride, as the long forks make low-speed maneuvers treacherous and the rigid frame makes any bump a literal pain in the...well, you get the point.

1-2. Sporting-goods manufacturer American Machine and Foundry (AMF) purchased Harley-Davidson in 1969, and promptly went about expanding the company's production—and markets. Harley's snowmobile, which came out in 1971, boasted some innovative features but didn't last long, succumbing after just five years. 3. Accessories remained a big part of Harley's profit picture; these gauges are just a small sample of the goodies available.

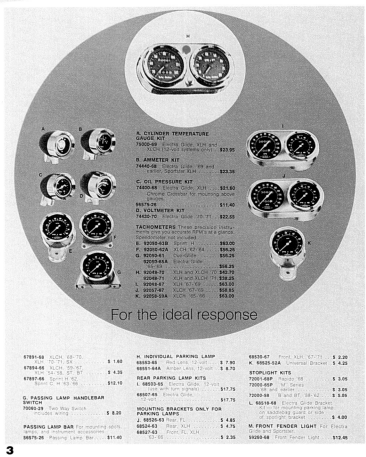

For the ideal response

1969

Looking like Harley's knight in shining armor, AMF plans a big increase in production; the down side, however, is a decrease in quality

Sprint engine grows from 250- to 350-cc for 1969, as street version takes on the name SS

1969 sees the debut of Honda's 750 Four, which is quicker, smoother, and far less expensive than Harley's Sportster

Other Japanese manufacturers join in, eroding Harley's traditional "big bike" customer base

Fulfilling President Kennedy's promise of putting a man on the moon by the end of the decade, Neil Armstrong makes "One small step for man, one giant leap for mankind" out of Apollo 11 on July 20, 1969

In the summer of 1969, about half-a-million people attend the Woodstock rock festival in New York state

1. Referred to in this promotion as "the entertainer," Evel Knievel made a career of jumping over all sorts of things in a single bound. 2. Combining the Big Twin (FL) engine and frame with the Sportster (XL) front end produced the Super Glide (FX), introduced in 1971. The original model came with drum brakes and a "boat-tail" rear fender, which many didn't like; by the mid-Seventies when this ad came out, disc brakes were fitted and a conventional rear fender was used. 3. There was a vast amount of memorabilia generated to promote stuntman Evel Knievel; this plastic and metal toy was one of the better examples. 4. A Harley brochure from 1971 lists a wide assortment of accessory seats, including the unpopular boat-tail seat/fender used on the 1970-71 Sportster.

the entertainer!

Just add ego. And go.

You've earned it.
Along with the right to deck yourself out however you please.
To be noticed. And remembered. In flamboyant style.
On the machine that's beyond all the rest.
FX-1200 Ego includes: 1200 cc's of power, exclusive hydraulic discs front and rear. Dual exhausts. Rakish new tank. Fantastic new suspension. Rocket Man. Freedom. All the way.

Harley-Davidson, Milwaukee, Wisconsin 53201
Member Motorcycle Industry Council

Harley-Davidson FX-1200.
The Great American Freedom Machine.

1

2

3

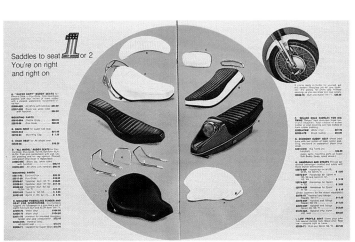

4

*L*ittle changed on the Sportster XLH for 1970; tank badges were the same, though the two-tone paint treatment differed somewhat. Sharp eyes will notice, however, that the left side engine cases now sported ribs, and the headlight "eyebrow" formerly exclusive to the XLCH now adorned the XLH as well. The two still differed, however, in that the XLCH carried a unique fuel tank and exhaust system, as well as a kickstarter instead of the XLH's electric leg. Formerly, the XLCH was fired by a magneto; for 1970, it switched to the timer and coil setup from the XLH.

1971
Baja 100

Harley-Davidson branched into yet another market in 1970 with the introduction of the MSR-100, better known as the Baja 100. With but six cubic inches displaced by its two-stroke engine, the Baja was no rocket, but its ample ground clearance, short wheelbase, and light weight made it fairly competitive in 100-cc dirt-bike competition, and it even won the famed Greenhorn Enduro one year. But the Baja 100 never really caught on with riders, most of whom gravitated toward its ever-improving Japanese rivals. Electric lighting was added as an option for 1972 in an effort to broaden its appeal, but annual production never topped 1500 units, and the Baja 100 (by now carrying the designation SR-100) bit the dust after 1974.

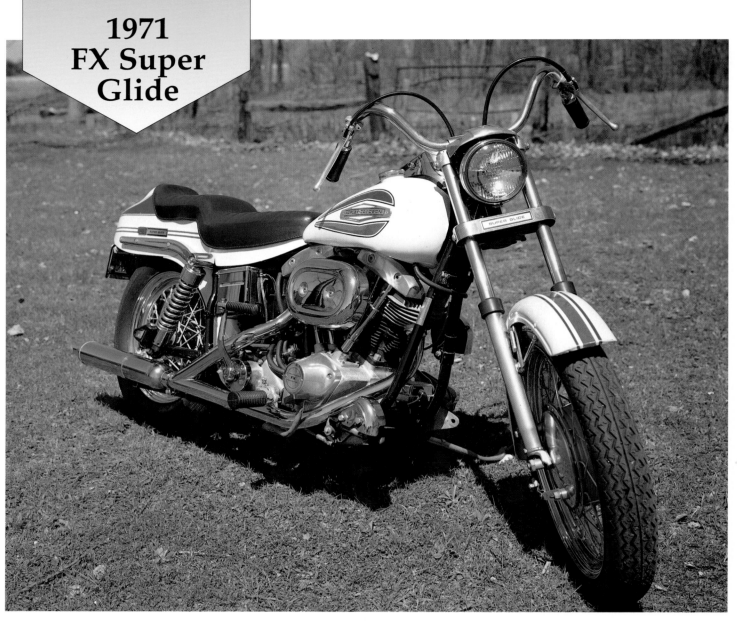

*C*ustomized motorcycles were all the rage by the early Seventies, but none of the various manufacturers ever offered one off the showroom floor—until Harley brought out the 1971 FX Super Glide. Mating the FL's Big Twin engine and frame with the XL Sportster's lighter front end (complete with "eyebrow" headlight cover) accounted for the FX designation, but it was the fiberglass boat-tail seat/fender combination and buckhorn handlebars that made it a Super Glide. Early Super Glides came only with kick starters; not until 1974 was an electric leg made available. Optional in its debut season was the Sparkling America paint treatment shown on our featured bike, the obvious choice for those patriotic souls who wanted to make a statement while riding the world's first factory custom.

*T*he fiberglass boat-tail rear fender that was introduced on the 1970 Sportster didn't meet with universal acceptance, so Harley reverted to a normal fender for 1971 and made the boat-tail a $60 option. Also optional was the Sparkling America paint scheme seen on the FX Super Glide, as well as several custom colors—one of which was the Sparkling Turquoise of our featured bike, which also sports the boat-tail fender. But none of these styling experiments met with much success, and they were all absent from the options list when the 1972 models debuted.

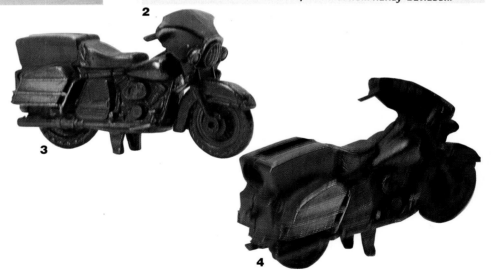

1. Harley ads in the early Seventies continued to push the touring capabilities of the big FLH. 2. For 1972, the Aermacchi-built Sprint engine found its way into a more modern frame, but it wouldn't be enough to save the bike from extinction. The ad touts its "four-stroke torque," something its two-stroke successor would have to debunk. 3-4. This tiny toy Harley is actually a pencil sharpener. It has remarkable detail considering it's only 1½-inches long.

1969 1970 1971	The 747 makes its first commercial flight in 1969, while the supersonic Concorde makes its first flight across the U.S., from Seattle to New York	Stuntman Evel Knievel starts his career jumping a modified XR-750 over cars, buses—anything he can find	Consumers give AMF/Harley-Davidson's new snowmobile, which was introduced in 1971, the cold shoulder; it lasts only through 1975
	For 1970, the XLCH discards its magneto ignition for the timer and coil setup from the XLH	Baja 100 dirt bike comes on board in 1970, but lasts only through '74	1971: The 26th Amendment is passed, allowing 18-year-olds to vote; Joe Frazier defeats Muhammad Ali for the heavyweight crown; The Beatles disband
	Harley's XR-750, in its first year of racing action in 1970, racks up an impressive string of victories	Harley's first factory custom, the FX Super Glide, debuts for 1971; it's not particularly popular, but the name—and the concept—would live on	

1

2

3

4

5

1-5. The diminutive Shortster marked a new "low" in Harley history. Though the 65-cc two-stroke minibike had the company's name stamped into its cases, the engine was built by Aermacchi, Harley's Italian partner. Minibikes didn't stay in the lineup for long; this example dates from 1972.

Over 70,000 Harleys left the factory in 1973, yet only a thousand or so were FLs; the high-compression FLH was far more popular. The Big Twins had gained a front disc brake for 1972, and this '73 shows off the new tank badge (incorporating the AMF logo) and bar-code style graphics. This unrestored example is loaded with extras, but got little use; There are only 68 original miles on the odometer.

**1973
X-90**

he X-90 was one of two minibikes offered by Harley-Davidson in 1973; the Z-90 differed only slightly, such as having fixed handlebars in lieu of the X-90's folding ones. Powered by a 90-cc two-stroke single, these minibikes came complete with speedometer and lights, and could be made street-legal. Ten-inch cast wheels incorporating drum brakes were mounted front and rear, and a protective metal leg shield covered the high-mounted muffler. Versatile as they were, production of these minibikes lasted only three years before Japanese competitors stole the show.

1. After better than 40 years on the market, the three-wheeled Servi-Car finally bit the dust after this 1973 model was built. It carried its original 45-cubic-inch flathead V-twin to the very end. 2. Published in 1974, this comic book was a joint venture between Marvel Comics and the Ideal Toy Company. 3. Harley-Davidson added an electric starter to the FX Super Glide in 1974 to make it the FXE, and model companies lost little time in offering hobbyists their own version. A ⅙th scale kit has been re-released by Tamiya.

1

2

3

1972 1973	The last U.S. ground troops are withdrawn from Vietnam, though bombing continues	FLs get a front disc brake for 1972	1973: All U.S. troops leave Vietnam; Watergate prosecution begins; Vice President Spiro Agnew resigns amid charges of corruption; Gerald Ford named vice president
	Five people are caught breaking into the Democratic Headquarters in the Watergate building; culprits are traced back to the Committee to Re-elect the President	XLs get a boost to 1000 ccs for 1972	
		Government makes turn signals mandatory in 1973	1973 OPEC oil embargo triggers large price increases and long lines at some gas stations
	Richard Nixon is re-elected president	XLs get front disc brakes for 1973	

1

2

3

1. This 1975 Sportster has been meticulously restored to its original splendor. Very few stock examples remain from this period in Harley's history. 2. A quartet of new 175- and 250-cc two-stroke singles were introduced in the mid-Seventies to replace the Aermacchi-built four-stroke singles. The road-going SS-250 came out in 1975, but none of the four lasted past 1978, as government emission standards were regulating two-strokes out of existence. 3. During the Seventies, the AMF badge—often accompanied by the corporation's red, white, and blue-striped logo—appeared on virtually every Harley product. Because many riders didn't like the connection, few bikes from this era escaped the customizer's touch.

One of four new two-stroke singles introduced by Harley-Davidson in the mid-Seventies, the SS-250 debuted in 1975 and was the largest street version offered. On/off-road models carried the SX prefix, and both bikes were eventually available in 175- and 250-cc sizes. The engine was based on a Yamaha design, but the Environmental Protection Agency was beginning to frown on all two-stroke bikes as a major source of pollution. Like most Harleys of the era, fuel tanks carried the AMF logo and corporate tri-colored striping theme.

*I*ntroduced in 1970 to replace the aging flathead-powered KR-750, the XR-750 carried Harley's competition banner to numerous dirt-track wins during the decade. Based on the Sportster V-twin, the engine originally carried iron cylinders and heads, which were replaced by aluminum components in 1972. At the same time, exhaust pipes, which at first exited low to the right side of the bike, were routed so that they exited high on the left side. In both cases, the rear cylinder's intake and exhaust valves switched positions from normal practice. Dual Mikuni carburetors fed the V-twin, and a mere quarter-turn of the throttle would raise their slides from idle position to wide open—at which point the rider was holding the reins on 90 thrashing horsepower. Not until the Japanese entered dirt-track racing with more sophisticated machinery late in the decade did the XR-750 fade from glory.

ONLY ONE MAN COULD HAVE DONE THIS.

Harley-Davidson's new Cafe Racer couldn't have been built by a committee. There's no compromise.

Only one man could have built the Cafe Racer. Willie G. If he wore a suit, he'd be William G. Davidson. But he doesn't. So he's Willie G., the man who designed the Super Glide, and now, the all-new, 1977 XLCR Cafe Racer.

"I wanted to build the ultimate, no compromise bike. So I built it first, then presented it. Before the presentation, I said to myself, "If they like it, we're going to build it. If they don't, I'll keep it for myself." They liked it.

No wonder. A street legal Cafe Racer in black on black, Willie G.'s creation may be the ultimate customizing job.

He took the engine from the powerful 1977 Sportster. Sculpted the seat and rear end to resemble the famous XR-750 racer. Added a specially-designed gas tank. Put on a unique Siamese exhaust system with all black pipes.

Those pipes, coupled with the Sportster engine, make the Cafe Racer the most powerful production cycle Harley-Davidson has ever built. Possessed with an ability to compete with the

best of Europe's Cafe Racers, it can handle down a twisting road while providing outstanding handling at high speeds.

And every detail, from the casting of aluminum cast wheels with Goodyear Eagle AT tires, to the positioning of the footpegs and the inclusion of low profile handlebars, the careful selection of Willie G.

You'll find dual front disc brakes, and a single rear disc brake in the rear. A blurred, sinister, black fairing with a smoke-colored

windshield. And everywhere there's black. Black frame, black covers, black tanks are cleaner cover and pipes. Even the return to cast of the amazing Harley-Davidson brake plate on the gas tank comes from the same source. "Who did I go to the old plant? I just like it."

Willie G. built himself a Cafe Racer. Now you can buy it. However, there will only be a limited number available. See your Harley-Davidson dealer for details.

Until you've been on a Harley-Davidson, you haven't been on a motorcycle.

Escape mechanism.

Move with a friend who mirrors your mind. Or alone...in a place where your thoughts are your own. Leggero. Your ticket away from a world you never made. AMF | Harley-Davidson, Milwaukee.

Leggero. 1 another outperformer from Harley-Davidson.

Cycle
1
Jay Springsteen
HARLEY-DAVIDSON
RIDER OF THE YEAR 1977

1. After his success with the Super Glide, William G. Davidson, grandson of one of the founders and head of Harley-Davidson styling, applied the currently popular "cafe-racer" look to a Sportster to come up with the XLCR for 1977. Production was limited and demand even more so; the experiment lasted only two years. 2. The Leggero was another Seventies attempt to sell a small two-stroke cycle to the beginning rider. The effort—quite predictably—proved futile. 3. One of racer Jay Springsteen's numerous accolades was winning *Cycle* magazine's Rider of the Year award in 1977—a year in which he campaigned a Harley XR-750. *Opposite page:* 1-2. Believe it or not, this isn't a real Harley; it's an incredibly detailed model of the 1976 Liberty Edition full-dresser made by The Franklin Mint.

1974 1975 1976	Aermacchi-built four-stroke horizontal single is replaced in 1974 by a variety of 175- and 250-cc two-stroke singles, also built with the help of Aermacchi; none would last past 1978, at which time Harley would abandon the small- and medium-sized markets to concentrate on big V-twins	FX Super Glide gains electric starting in 1974 to become the FXE 55-mph speed limit is instituted in 1974 1974: President Richard Nixon resigns from office amid threats of impeachment; he is replaced by Vice President Ford, who grants him a full pardon	Sportster adopts left-side shift for 1975 Muhammad Ali regains the heavyweight title from Joe Frazier in the "Thrilla in Manila" Celebrating America's bicentennial in 1976, Harley introduces five "Liberty Editions" trimmed in gold

*H*arley-Davidson dabbled in numerous markets during the AMF years, but few probably anticipated the appearance of a motocross machine. Motocross racing had only recently been sanctioned by the American Motorcycle Association when Harley hit the tracks with the Aermacchi-built MX250 in 1977. It carried a single-cylinder two-stroke engine, chrome-moly frame, Japanese-made forks, and remote-reservoir rear shocks. Almost surprisingly, it was quite competitive—right up until the Japanese attacked the market with cheaper, faster entries. So rapid was this invasion that the MX250 lasted only two years.

*I*n an attempt to capitalize on the cafe-racing trend that was sweeping the country in the mid-Seventies, Harley-Davidson ventured back into the world of customs to bring out the XLCR. Styled by William "Willie G." Davidson, it applied a small "bikini" fairing, skimpy front fender, angular fuel tank, solo seat with fiberglass tail section, triple disc brakes, and special "siamesed" two-into-two exhaust headers to a standard Sportster, and then cloaked the whole affair in black. Problem was that although the XLCR was claimed to be "the most powerful production cycle Harley-Davidson has ever built," that wasn't saying much; Japanese competitors were quite a bit faster and cheaper to boot. Furthermore, the typical Harley buyer seemed to take little interest in joining the road-racing crowd, so sales never took off, and what was in fact a very interesting motorcycle (and quite soon, a very *collectible* motorcycle) faded away after only two years.

A long with the radical XLCR cafe racer came another factory custom for 1977, the FXS Low Rider. More in tune with Harley rider's tastes, the FXS cruiser proved an instant hit, outselling all other models in the line. A matte-black instrument panel perched atop wide "Fat Bob" fuel tanks, while low handlebars and a very low stepped seat combined to give it a dragster look. Both kick and electric starters were provided to bring the 74-cubic-inch Big Twin to life, and nine-spoke cast wheels held triple disc brakes. Originally offered only in metallic gray, black and white were added later in the year. The FXS changed little for 1978, though that would prove to be the final year for the 74-inch version of the Big Twin.

1

1. To celebrate the company's 75th anniversary in 1978, Harley built a limited number of specially equipped XL-1000 Sportsters with gold trim and a leather saddle. 2. The Matchbox Company produced many Harley replicas over the years. This one, released in 1980, has the look of a contemporary FL.

2

1976	Jimmy Carter is elected U.S. president	Sidecar fans lose the three-speed plus reverse transmission option in 1977	Sportsters get electronic ignition for 1978
1977	The Apple "personal" computer is developed	1977: The first Space Shuttle is tested	Leon Spinks wins—and then loses—the heavyweight crown in separate matches with Muhammad Ali
1978			
1979	1977 brings two new customs: the FXS Low Rider and the XLCR; the former would go on to fame and fortune, the latter would soon slip into oblivion	An 80-cubic-inch V-twin returns as an option to power the 1978 Electra Glide	Lower-powered FL dropped for 1979

1

2

3

1-2. Introduced for 1983 in very limited numbers was the potent XR-1000, as close to a racing bike for the street as Harley ever produced. With its aluminum heads, twin Dell'Orto carbs, and high-mounted left-side dual exhausts, its association with the racing XR-750 was obvious. Sadly, it was only offered for a couple of years, assuring its stature as a collectible. 3. The Heirloom Collectors Guild released this limited-edition replica of an early Harley in 1980. Crafted from sterling silver and gold, it is astoundingly accurate in detail.

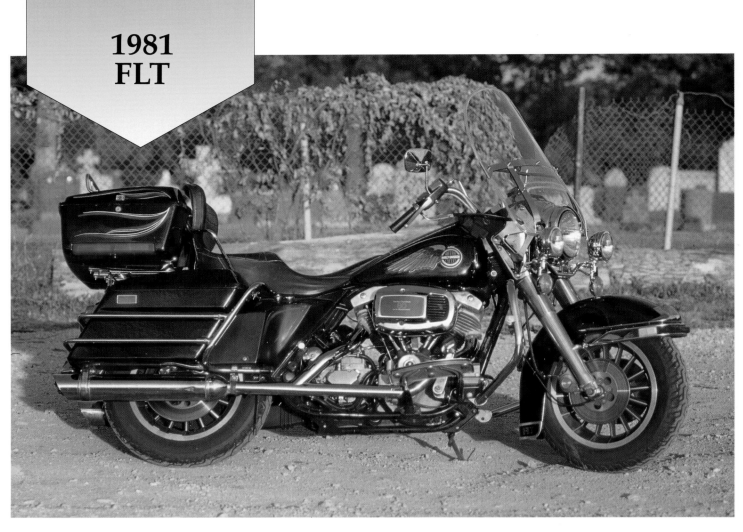

1981
FLT

hough relatively few were built, the FLT was considered a favorite among those who spent long hours on the road. Beneath the winged Harley-Davidson tank decal—which for the first time in a long while was devoid of the AMF logo—sat a large new air cleaner that graced many of the early-Eighties V-twins. Adding a Tour Pack trunk to the traditional skirted fenders, windshield, and hard-sided saddlebags, the FLT's only telltale badging appeared on the lower front fender guard *(opposite page, bottom right)*.

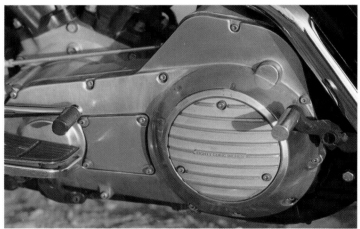

1. He's hardly the person you'd expect to see on a chopper, yet theeeeeeere's Ed. Actually, Ed McMahon starred with numerous other Hollywood types in an Eighties comedy called *Gridlock*, later retitled *The Great American Traffic Jam.* Note that the bike is strapped down to a trailer. 2. Harley's popularity among law-enforcement agencies waned during the Seventies and Eighties, but here an Oakland police officer is seen straddling a 1979 FLH. 3. Even the Avon cosmetics firm got into the cycle act with this decanter modeled after a three-wheeled chopper. Twisting off the front end revealed the scent of a "Sure Winner." *Opposite page:* 1-2. This highly detailed ⅛th scale replica of a circa 1983 FLT comes pre-assembled. Made up of over 700 parts—most of them metal—it is a substantial piece that weighs five-and-a-half pounds.

1

2

3

1979	The Three Mile Island nuclear plant in Pennsylvania suffers a meltdown in 1979
1980	
1981	Second Gas Crisis occurs
1982	U.S. Embassy in Iran is seized in the fall of 1979; 62 American hostages are held for more than a year
1983	

Ronald Reagan is elected U.S. president in 1980

1981: Harley management joins together to buy The Motor Company back from AMF

FXRs are introduced late in 1981 with five-speed gearboxes and rubber-mounted drive-trains

Sportster gets a stronger frame for 1982, along with a 25th anniversary model

1983 brings the Sportster XLX-61, a stripped price-leader, along with the exotic XR-1000, a street version of the racing XR-750

1

2

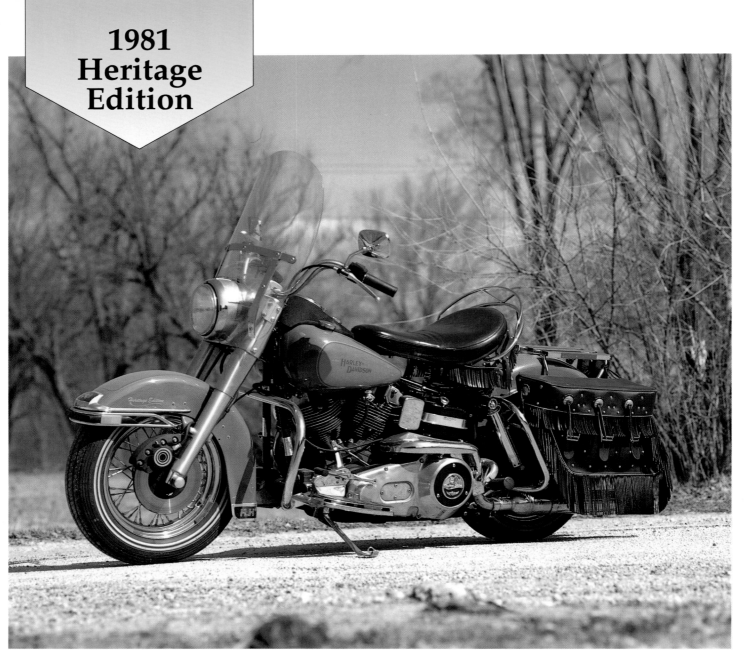

*W*ith its skirted fenders, Sixties-style headlight bezel, twin chrome-covered rear shocks, classic Buddy Seat with grab rail, and fringed seat and saddlebags, the 1981 Heritage Edition lived up to its name. Even the rather odd Olive Green and orange paint job struck a chord of years past. The Heritage was one of the first Harley creations to combine the new 80-cubic-inch V-twin—not seen since the Forties—with the retro look; something that is today a standard commodity in Harley's lineup.

*I*ntroduced in 1982, the FXB was known as the Sturgis, as its first public showing was in Sturgis, South Dakota, during the week-long motorcycle extravaganza held there each summer. The FX nomenclature identifies it as a version of the Low Rider; the B suffix, however, means that it is driven by belts—both primary (engine to transmission) and secondary (transmission to rear wheel)—rather than conventional chains. Completing the factory custom look were extended forks, buckhorn handlebars, stepped king/queen seat, and black paint—acres of it—with just a touch of chrome and orange trim. Popular from the start, the FXB quickly became a modern classic.

MONEY IN THE BANK.

When you buy a Harley-Davidson® motorcycle you own what motorcyclists everywhere recognize as the finest piece of real motorcycle iron there is.

You own more than a machine. You own a reputation. You own what Harley riders affectionately call...a Hog.

Now putting your money into a Hog is not like putting your money into some ordinary motorcycle. We put more into a Harley. So you get more out of a Harley.

You get more every time you ride down the street. And more down the road, when it comes time to sell. Just check the want ads. You'll be in Hog Heaven.

You see, a Harley may be called a Hog, but don't be confused. There's no better place to put your money.

1

1. For 1983, Harley-Davidson stressed the investment potential of its motorcycles, saying "Just check the want ads." Today's newspapers bear out the accuracy of that financial wisdom, as late Shovelheads often command nearly their original price. 2. Not only is Martin Jack Rosenblum a successful songwriter and poet, he is also Harley-Davidson's archivist. 3. This glass mug is adorned with a reproduction of a Harley-Davidson oil can label—though it's doubtful that holding oil is its intended use.

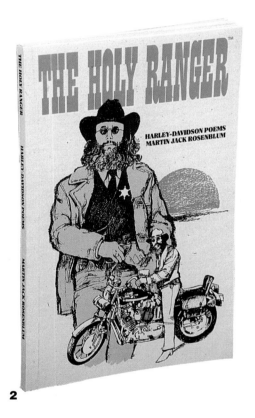

2

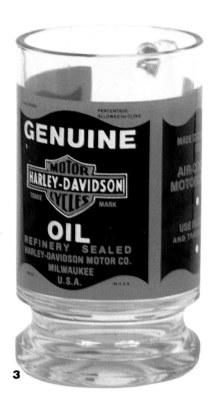

3

1983

The Harley Owners Group (H.O.G.) is formed in 1983 to unite riders from around the world

Harley's comeback prompts Japanese manufacturers to mimic the company's offerings; imitation may be the sincerest form of flattery, but some Japanese bikes are virtual copies

At Harley's prompting, a tariff is imposed on all foreign motorcycles over 700 ccs in April, 1983; initial tariff is stiff, but is set to decline—and eventually fade away—over the next few years

Japanese manufactures avoid the tariff on many models by reducing engine size to just below the 700-cc limit

U.S. Embassy in Beirut, Lebanon, is bombed in April, 1983, Marine barracks are hit by truck bomb in October

U.S. invades the island of Granada in October, 1983 after a Marxist coup overthrows the government

1983 MOTORCYCLES. BY THE PEOPLE. FOR THE PEOPLE.™

© Harley-Davidson

© Harley-Davidson

© Harley-Davidson

1. Under a slogan paraphrasing a famous line from Abraham Lincoln's Gettysburg Address, Harley's 1983 catalog listed no fewer than eleven different models--and that number would grow in subsequent years. 2. Custom Big Twins accounted for nearly half the motorcycles offered by the company in '83. Anchoring the line was the FXE Super Glide, riding the older frame and being equipped with solid-mounted engine and four-speed gearbox. 3. Like the FXE, the FXSB Low Rider was built on the "old" frame, but added primary and secondary belts in place of chains. It also sported mag wheels instead of spokes along with tank-mounted instruments. 4. With its chopper-style wide-spaced forks and bucket headlight, Harley called the FXWG Wide Glide the "one custom motorcycle [that] goes all out." Like the other FX models with the older-style frame, seat heights were about two inches lower than on the FXR models with the new frame. 5. When the FXR debuted in 1982, it was heralded as a landmark motorcycle for Harley-Davidson. Its new frame was not only stiffer, it also incorporated isolated engine mounts that quelled some of the V-twin's numbing vibration. Further enhancing highway travel was a five-speed gearbox. Its FXRS sibling traded spoked wheels for mags, and added some other custom touches. FXR models can be differentiated by the triangular-shaped frame member beneath the seat and the rear-set shocks in back. They also carried both handlebar- and tank-mounted gauges.

© Harley-Davidson

© Harley-Davidson

269

THE EVOLUTION REVOLUTION

Ask ten Shovelhead owners whether they like their bikes, and all will likely give a resoundingly positive response. But ask ten *former* Shovelhead owners whether they liked their bikes, and you'll probably get different reactions altogether. Why the discrepancy? First of all, few people will berate what they currently own. Secondly, most old-time Harley riders are used to vibration and the more-than-occasional breakdown—to them, that's just part of owning a Harley-Davidson. If you've never tasted filet mignon, hamburger will suit you just fine.

When Harley-Davidson introduced the Evolution V2 on some 1984 models, skeptics questioned not so much whether it was an improvement (most felt it had to be), but whether it was improved enough to rival the Japanese V-twins. The cylinders, now aluminum, enclosed the same 80 cubic inches as before, but new heads provided a higher compression ratio while being perfectly contented with regular unleaded gas. Per Harley practice, the valve covers were altered in design, this time displaying smooth, billet-like contours that soon had enthusiasts calling it the Blockhead. Computers were used in the design process, and the end result was an engine that was smoother, quieter, more powerful, and—as time would tell—far more reliable.

Oddly, not every 1984 Big Twin got the Evo engine, and some that did continued with solid engine mounts and a four-speed transmission (isolated mounts and a five-speed had both been offered on some models in the early Eighties). Those that stuck with the Shovelhead all had solid mounts and a four-speed transmission, so there was a wide variety of powertrain choices available.

Those trying to keep the various models straight were faced with an almost impossible task by this time. Sportsters (XL) weren't too hard to keep track of, since minor styling details and equipment levels differentiated most of the bikes. The sole mechanical variation could be found on the exotic XR-1000 introduced in 1983, which carried a dual-carb, aluminum-head engine based on the one used for the XR-750 racer. Big Twins, however, were another story. By now, they could generally be divided into three categories: FL (touring bikes); FX (customs); and FXR (sport/touring).

Within the various categories some acronyms stood out. ST meant Softail, an innovative Harley frame design that looked like the hardtail frames of old, but provided a comforting amount of rear suspension. Introduced along with the Evolution engine in 1984, it has since spread to numerous FL and FX models. STS meant a Softail frame combined with a Springer front fork, which again recalled the look of yesteryear while improving upon its capabilities. WG designated the *Wide Glide*, an FX with widely spaced forks, though those forks were also used on other FX models that didn't carry the *WG* nomenclature. Other than that, there weren't many firm rules.

Making matters worse is that, as indicated previously, not all innovations were found on all bikes at the same time. A five-speed transmission and isolated engine mounts were used on some models of a given year, but not others. Triple disc brakes weren't always universal, and only certain models were blessed with the anti-dive forks introduced on the FXRS of 1983.

The Evolution revolution caught up with the Sportster in 1986, the former 1000-cc engine being replaced by a pair of Evos measuring 883- and 1100-ccs. The latter eventually grew to 1200 ccs, which incidently equates to 74 cubic inches, the same size as the old Big Twin. Sportster choices have expanded of late; for 1996, the tally rests at five.

But the bottom line to all this is that the Evolution models were a greatly improved breed, and today exhibit a level of quality and refinement that wouldn't have been dreamed of by Harley riders of old. Which brings us back to those ten riders who don't miss their Shovelheads.

They're riding Evos.

HARLEY-DAVIDSON 1984. COMING ON STRONG.

...tion is
...than
...testimony to
...there's more to a motor-
...designed to
...from Point A to Point B.
...the way is a new and
...V-Twin, our V² Evolu-
...Engine. Not a revolutionary
...from past Harley traditions,
...refinement of Milwaukee V-Twin
...A technological wonder that
...out: 10% more horsepower, 15%
...re torque and outstanding gas
...age. In five years and 750,000
...s of testing, the V²™ test engines
...e proven low in maintenance, high
...durability and absolutely tight as a
...m in oil-sealing properties.
   We're racing into 1984 with our
...eatest statement of street savvy

...ever. We turned our racing department
loose on the streets and they returned
with the XR-1000, a pavement
burner that begs to be opened up.
   We're setting new standards in
custom design with the introduction of

the new FXST Softail.™ A distinctly
American factory custom bike that

sits just 25¼" off the ground. A classic
remake of the Harley-Davidson hardtail

of years past, with a style and
suspension design that's years ahead.
   We're taking the roadshow on
tour this year with our strongest line-

up of touring bikes since William
Harley and Arthur Davidson first put
pen to paper in 1903. Leading the
pack is our new FXRT Sport Glide,™ a
down-to-earth sport tourer that take
the technology out of the cockpit an
puts it beneath you, where you need
it most.
   These are motorcycles crafted
by the people who know and ride
motorcycles. People who have measured the pulse of the rider and have
responded in kind. People committe
to designing bikes that don't pass
into obsolescence the next year.
   There's never been a better tim
to experience what motorcycling wa
meant to be. Harley-Davidson for
1984. Motorcycles by the people, for
the people.

© Harley-Davidson

1984 HARLEY-DAVIDSON® MOTORCYCLES.

HARLEY-DAVIDSON
MOTOR COMPANY

Harley-Davidson

© Harley-Davidson

1. Still displacing the same 80 cubic inches as the later Shovelheads, 1984's Evolution V-twin was nonetheless a much more refined powerplant. Its smooth, angular valve-cover design earned it the nickname "Blockhead," but most owners referred to it as the Evo. Oddly, only certain 1984 Big Twins got it: both FXRs, two of three FLs, and the new FXST were the fortunate ones, as the others stuck with the Shovelhead for one more year. 2. While picturesque, Harley's 1984 brochure cover gave little hint as to the revolution taking place within Big Twin frame rails. Inside, it also made little mention of the FXST's new Softail frame, which looked like the hardtail frames of old, yet incorporated modern rear suspension technology.

1984

Evolution engine introduced on some Big Twins in 1984

Seven years in the making, the Evo allows engineers to correct some of the flaws that plagued the Shovelhead design

New engine displaces 80 cubic inches, and some models boast rubber mounts to quell vibration, as well as a five-speed transmission

In a banner year for The Motor Company, 1984 also brings a new Softail frame on the FXST that looks like the hardtail frames of old, yet incorporates a triangulated rear swingarm with suspension components hidden under the bike

1. The three-model Sportster line once again started with the stripped-down XLX-61, little changed from 1983. It would be another couple of years before Sportsters got their own Evolution engine. 2. The up-scale XLH carried the same mechanicals as the XLX, but added a dual seat, buckhorn handlebars, and some polished trim pieces. 3. Never a big seller, the racer-like XR-1000 carried on for 1984 with its performance-modified twin-carb engine, but otherwise looked like the base XLX. It came only in Slate Gray.

4. Leading off for the Big Twins was the FXE Super Glide, still carrying a solid-mounted Shovelhead engine and four-speed transmission. 5. The base FLH Electra Glide was the only one of Harley's touring bikes to stick with the Shovelhead engine, solid engine mounts, and four-speed transmission. Its only claim to modern technology was belt drive. 6. With Evolution power, isolated engine mounts, and five-speed transmission, the FLHTC Electra Glide Classic was at the other end of the scale. However, it swapped belt drive for an oil-bath enclosed chain.

1. For 1985, Harley's Low Glide gained belt drive, but otherwise came with all the goodies it had offered before: a stiffer frame that provided better handling, isolated engine mounts, and five-speed transmission. It also carried the Evolution engine, but so did all Big Twins for 1985. 2. Harley's belt drive was proving both popular and reliable, so more and more of its big bikes were getting it. This page in the brochure described the advantages.

© Harley-Davidson

To destroy a few myths about shaft drive, here's an exploded view of our belt.

In recent years, there has been a transformation in motorcycle drive systems. A steady movement away from chain drive, primarily in the touring and custom categories.

Some manufacturers have switched their motorcycles to shaft drive, proclaiming its indestructible nature as state-of-the-art motorcycle technology.

But take a closer look. We did, over 40 years ago. We built a shaft drive motorcycle in 1942. That experience convinced us that shaft drive does not belong on a motorcycle. It's not worth the sacrifice in performance and handling.

At Harley-Davidson® we still believe that form follows function. And in our experience, a more functional drive system for the modern American motorcycle is one built into the very first motorcycles—belt drive.

Not the leather belts used earlier this century. Rather, tough-as-steel aramid fiber composition belts.

The Harley-Davidson belt drive system is a product of American

ingenuity. Built by motorcyclists, for motorcyclists. Here are its advantages.

Belt drive is more efficient than a shaft.

Engineering data show that belt drive transmits an unbeatable 99% of the engine's power. Shaft drive, on the other hand, saps 7-10% of the engine power.

It's been reported that, to compensate for this power loss, some manufacturers have had to boost engine displacement in their shaft drive models just to make performance equal to a chain.

Belt drive handles better than a shaft.

The ring-and-pinion in the rear wheel of a shaft drive machine transmits a torque reaction that jacks the back end up and down with every twist of the throttle.

Even on straight, perfectly paved roads, shaft drive is unacceptable. As you close the throttle, a shaft-driven bike sinks on its suspension. That reduces ground clearance, for an uncomfortable if not scary ride, especially around corners and over bumps.

Belt drive is just as clean as a shaft.

A belt requires absolutely no lubrication. In addition, after initial break-in, it can go up to 8,000 miles before it needs adjustment.

Belt drive is lighter weight than a shaft.

Shaft drive makes a motorcycle noticeably heavier, especially in back. The extra weight reduces payload and acceleration.

Belt drive is less complicated than a shaft.

No extra gears means smoother, quieter riding.

Belt drive is featured on all 1985 Harley-Davidson touring motorcycles—the Sport Glide,™ the Electra Glide,® and the Tour Glide.® In the custom category

belt drive is on the Low Rider,™ the Wide Glide,® and is a new feature on the 1985 Low Glide.™

In the showroom or out on the road, a close look reveals major differences between belt drive and shaft drive. When it comes to

choosing between the two, go with the one that belongs on a motorcycle. Belt drive.

© Harley-Davidson

1984 1985 1986

Along with a virtual explosion of growth in the accessory market, clothing continues to be a hot seller for Harley dealers

The last Shovelhead engine is produced in June of 1984

"New Coke" is introduced in 1985; it fails in the marketplace, prompting the return of the original formula, now called "Coca-Cola Classic"

Sportsters gain their own version of the Evolution engine in 1986, offered in 883- and 1100-cc displacements; it has aluminum heads and cylinders, and hydraulic lifters, but still only a four-speed transmission

1. Harley's 1985 brochure identified its three markets: Street, represented by a Sportster; Custom, illustrated by a Softail; and Touring, depicted with a Sport Glide. Oddly, Harley dropped most model designations this year, going only with names—at least in the brochure. 2. Though most of Harley's offerings were Big Twins, Sportsters were still popular. The line again consisted of four models, led once more by the stripper XLX-61. 3. Last year's XLS Roadster was now simply called the Roadster. Though a Sportster model, it carried the Fat Bob tank with instrument panel as found on the custom Big Twins.

ot only was the FLSTC a popular choice among Harley enthusiasts, it was also chosen as the subject of a Franklin Mint replica in 1994. With retro styling that dated back to the early Hydra-Glide days, it featured the *de rigueur* softail frame and beefy FL telescopic forks combined with Fifties-style fenders. The seat and saddle bags were dressed with studs and decorative conchos, and fender-tip lights were fitted front and rear.

1988
FXSTS

*W*ith softail rear end and springer front forks, the FXSTS boasted a retro look but with modern mechanicals like front and rear disc brakes, a shock absorber for the front suspension, and belt final drive. Custom touches included a bobbed rear fender, chrome plating for the forks, and Fat Bob tanks with chromed instrument panel. The FXSTS was one of three Harley models chosen to wear special 85th anniversary graphics and badges in 1988.

1

2

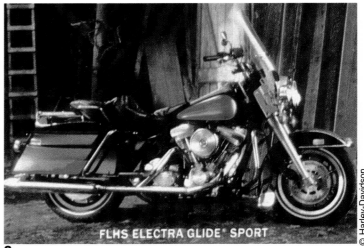

3

1. Harley's 1989 brochure cover gave more than a hint of the company's latest "Back to the Future" technology. Reintroduced the previous year on the FXSTS, springer forks hadn't been seen on Big Twins since 1948. 2. The 1989 FLSTC Heritage Softail Classic combined the Softail frame with time-honored Harley styling elements like FL forks with upper fork cover and skirted fenders. 3. Seemingly a contradiction in terms, the FLHS Electra Glide Sport for 1989 traded its traditional handlebar-mounted fairing for a simple windshield. Guess that's what made it so *sporty*.

1986

Harley-Davidson purchases RV manufacturer Holiday Rambler in 1986

In January of 1986, the space shuttle *Challenger* explodes shortly after take-off, killing all seven astronauts aboard

The Chernobyl nuclear power plant in Russia suffers a melt-down in April of 1986, resulting in major radioactive fallout

An illegal $30 million weapons sale to Iran sees the money diverted to help the Contras; government official Oliver North is implicated in the 1986 incident

FLTC ULTRA CLASSIC TOUR GUIDE®

1

© Harley-Davidson

FLHTC ULTRA CLASSIC ELECTRA GLIDE®

2

© Harley-Davidson

FLHTC ELECTRA GLIDE® CLASSIC

3

© Harley-Davidson

FLTC TOUR GLIDE® CLASSIC

4

© Harley-Davidson

1. Harley's top-line tourer, the FLTC Ultra Classic Tour Glide, differed from the Electra Glides in that it had a frame-mounted fairing with twin headlights. 2. When you've said "FLHTC Ultra Classic Electra Glide," you've said a mouthful. By now, all touring bikes had the isolated-mounted Evo engine, five-speed transmission, and belt drive, so the various models mostly differed only in degree of luxury. 3-4. Take away the CB/intercom, cruise control, and cigarette lighter, and you take away the "Ultra." The FLHTC Electra Glide Classic and FLTC Tour Glide Classic didn't seem to suffer much from the omissions. 5. The FXRS Low Rider combined the modern FXR chassis with a chrome-accented Evolution V-twin in wrinkle-finish black. 6. A Sport edition of the Low Rider offered dual front discs and anti-dive forks.

5

© Harley-Davidson

FXRS-SP LOW RIDER™ SPORT EDITION

6

© Harley-Davidson

1. This ceramic decanter was fired in 1988 to help celebrate the 85th anniversary of the Harley-Davidson Motor Company. 2. *Harley Rider* comic book was published in 1988; though intended as a series, it lasted only one issue. 3. One indication that the company's products have become more competitive is the fact that many police departments are once again riding Harleys. The California Highway Patrol ordered up a batch of FXRPs in the mid-Eighties.

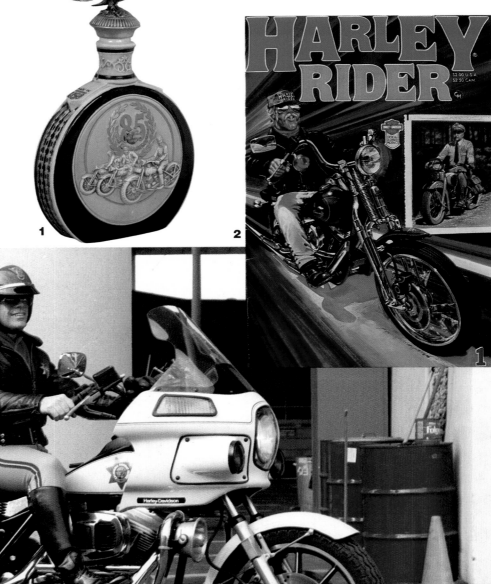

1

2

3

1987 1988

In the spring of 1987, Harley-Davidson requests an early repeal of the 1983 tariff aimed at foreign bikes over 700 ccs

Once again changing its ownership status, Harley-Davidson stock goes public on the New York Stock Exchange in July of 1987

After raising nearly $70 million through stock offerings, The Motor Company attacks the market with new models

George Bush is elected president in 1988

1

1. The Franklin Mint issued a meticulously detailed model of the 1988 FLHTC. 2-3. A collectible plate released in 1990 commemorates Elvis Presley. The back carries a serial number and assurances of limited edition status. 4. *Twin Peaks* attained cult status as a TV series in the early Nineties. James Hurley, played by James Marshall, is about to ride off from his uncle's gas station on his Harley.

2

3

4

The last time Harley-Davidson produced a commemorative Sturgis model there had been a Shovelhead engine nestled in the frame; the 1991 FXDB, of course, was powered by the Evolution V-twin—and that engine rested in a new Dynaglide chassis. The special Sturgis model marked the 50th anniversary of the famed Black Hills rally held every summer in Sturgis, South Dakota. As with the first Sturgis built in 1982, the paint scheme centered around black with orange trim—Harley's corporate colors.

1

3

4

2

© Harley-Davidson

1988
1989

Use of the Softail frame expands to several models

Harley brings back springer front forks on the custom FXSTS

Last seen on Big Twins in the Forties, the new springer forks offer double the wheel travel of the old design

Harley's 1989 lineup includes 19 different models

The Soviets withdraw forces from Afghanistan in 1989; the first sign that the USSR is softening its hard-line positions

1

Opposite page: 1. Arnold Schwarzenegger returned in *Terminator 2*, this time playing a *good* guy. He rides a Harley in an escape scene—and also in real life. 2. The 1992 Sportster 883 Hugger differed from the base model in that it added buckhorn handlebars and a lower suspension. 3. Harleys have long been subjects of the custom touch; the FLSTN "Cow Glide" came from the factory with bovine accents, but this owner gave it a few more. 4. Harley's 90th anniversary celebration, held in Milwaukee in the summer of 1993, included a two-and-a-half-hour parade, where riders shook hands with those who turned out to watch. *This page:* 1. Harley's management team poses for a portrait at the 90th. 2. A two-toned paint scheme and commemorative badges were applied to special 1993 models. 3. The celebration's parade brought out enthusiasts of all descriptions—and backed up traffic for miles.

WE'VE SURVIVED FOUR WARS, A DEPRESSION, A FEW RECESSIONS, SIXTEEN U.S. PRESIDENTS, FOREIGN AND DOMESTIC COMPETITION, RACETRACK COMPETITION, AND ONE MARLON BRANDO MOVIE. SOUNDS LIKE PARTY TIME TO US.

2

3

C ertainly one of the more outrageous special editions produced by the factory was the 1993 FLSTN, often called the "Cow Glide"—for obvious reasons. Like most of Harley's customs of the period, it carried the Softail frame and belt drive, but differed from the FX specials by utilizing the FL's heavy telescopic forks and retro-look skirted fenders. With its black and white paint and unique bovine trim (even the gas tank and saddle bags carried a hint of heifer), the FLSTN was an instant hit—and an instant sellout. Built only in 1993, just 2,700 copies were produced, insuring the model's status as a future collectible.

Harley-Davidson celebrated its 90th anniversary in 1993, and as might be expected, several models came dressed for the occasion with badges and plaques proclaiming their special place in history. One was the FXDWG Wide Glide. Introduced in 1980, the Wide Glide originally got its name from its widely spaced fork tubes, but also came with a 21-inch front wheel, high pull-back handlebars, forward-mounted foot pegs, bobbed rear fender, and a Fat Bob fuel tank sprayed with flames. All those features remained for 1993 except for the last; the Wide Glide came to the anniversary celebration in a two-tone silver tuxedo.

1

2

3

1989

The *Exxon Valdez* spills 11 million gallons of oil into Alaska's Prince William Sound in March, 1989

Hundreds of students are killed by the Chinese army at the Tiananmen Square Massacre in June of 1989

Poland ends 40 years of communist rule in August; other communist countries follow in its footsteps

1

2

3

4

Opposite page: 1. Though the Harley-Davidson story started in Milwaukee, the main manufacturing site is now located in York, Pennsylvania. 2. The Harley-lover's paradise also houses the official museum.
3. There's not much question as to the ownership of the structure. *This page:* 1-2. Two displays show the complex painting process used on each motorcycle.
3. Three former "Ms. Harley-Davidson" winners gathered at the 90th anniversary celebration in 1993. The company no longer bestows such an honor.
4. Colorado senator Ben Nighthorse Campbell (in flamed shirt) is an active motorcyclist.

1

2

1. The Plymouth Wisconsin Fairgrounds hosts a vintage class race each summer; contestants lined up for a photo at a recent outing. 2. The competition isn't intense, but the race is highly entertaining. An old Harley WR is seen tackling a corner. 3. This sterling silver pendant might lay claim to being the world's smallest Harley. 4. What the well-dressed rider wears for a night out on the town: This Harley tie clip and matching set of cufflinks can dress up any outfit.

3

4

San Francisco is rocked by an earthquake measuring 7.1 on the Richter scale in October of '89; it's the worst since 1906

East Germany begins issuing exit visas in November, 1989; the Berlin Wall, constructed in 1961, is demolished by joyous people from both East and West Germany

U.S. invades Panama

1990: USSR begins withdrawing troops from Czechoslovakia; Soviet leaders vote in February to abandon communism

1

2

3

1. Hillclimbing is still popular, and requires highly specialized equipment to win. This is the National Champion cycle for 1994. 2. A strong pot of Harley-Davidson coffee may be just the thing to kick-start your morning. 3. Tractor pulls attract a variety of strange machines, including this one powered by twin Harley engines.

*N*ot all riders like to feel the wind in their face; the FLHTC Ultra was built for those who prefer the luxury of a full-dressed machine. With its plush two-place saddle, electronic cruise control, CB radio, AM/FM cassette player, and cavernous saddlebags and trunk, the Ultra truly lives up to its name. It's the perfect mount for those who like to travel without forfeiting the comforts of home.

1

2

3

1. By pushing a button on the trunk, this battery-operated full dresser "revs" its engine, vibrates, and flashes its lights. 2. Revell released this well-detailed 1/8th scale model in 1995. 3. Cast figurines are common collectibles. Here an aging craftsman is striving to make some young Harley fan very happy.

1990 1991

East and West Germany unite

South Africa abolishes apartheid

Harley dealerships begin to get a new look for the '90s; modern design and neon lights welcome prospective buyers

Iraqi troops invade Kuwait in August of 1990; the action is criticized by the United Nations, and U.S. troops are moved in to begin Operation Desert Shield

On January 17, 1991, the U.S. begins bombing Iraq; Operation Desert Storm starts in February, and Iraq surrenders four days later

1

KID'S DINNERWARE SET

2

INFANT APPAREL SET

3

HARLEY-DAVIDSON

4

1. Biketoberfest of 1994 was used as the kickoff date for the opening of Daytona Harley-Davidson in Florida. 2. Kids can share their folk's enthusiasm with their own Harley collectibles. This five-piece dinnerware set came out in 1995. 3. Even *infants* can join in—but it would seem as though a piglet would have been a more fitting mascot. 4. More of an adult toy is this Harley telephone. The horn honks and the headlight flashes when you get a call.

1. The recent craze in trading cards did not go unnoticed at Harley-Davidson, and several sets of collectible cards appeared in the early Nineties. 2. There is seldom a lack of creativity in the world of motorcycling, as shown by this sidecan...er...*car*. 3. Harley-Davidson licensed this scale model semi tractor-trailer rig, which was limited to only 50,000 copies. 4. Yet another creative idea from Milwaukee is this radio/flashlight combination. Twist the hand grip, and it emits a revving sound.

1992 **1993**	Harley-Davidson Motorclothes are given their own catalog and presented in an upscale fashion	Special Edition designs flourish, many becoming collectible before they even hit the showroom floor	Terrorists bomb the World Trade Center in New York in February 1993
	1992: Bill Clinton is elected president	Johnny Carson tapes his last *Tonight Show*	Summer floods ravage the midwest in 1993

1

2

3

1. Dressed in denim jeans and leather cap and vest, this stuffed hog is the perfect gift for the young Harley enthusiast. 2. Reaching even further into the toy market is this Harley train set, a new version of which is released every year. 3. *Road Songs* is a two-disc CD set released by Harley-Davidson, complete with leather-bound carrying case. 4. This "Buffalo Glide" is often ridden (herded?) to major motorcycling events.

1995 FXSTSB

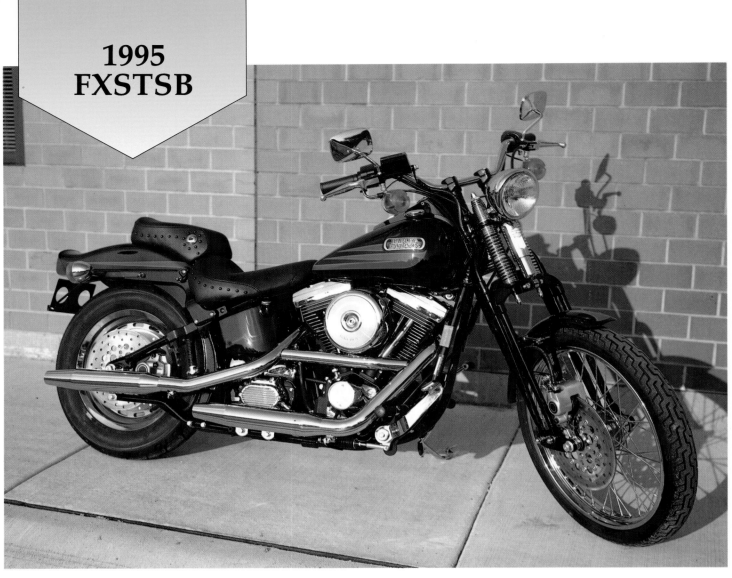

*Y*et another factory custom was the Bad Boy, which Harley brought to market in 1995. Unlike the Softail Springer on which it was based, the Bad Boy was cloaked in black, from the front fork to the bobbed rear fender, though numerous trim pieces were given the chrome treatment. Up front was a 21-inch spoked wheel carrying a drilled disc brake, while a drilled disc was also fitted to the solid rear wheel. Low handlebars stretched the rider out a bit, as did the high-mounted foot pegs. Carried over virtually unchanged for 1996, the Bad Boy is one sinister ride.

1995
Drag Bike

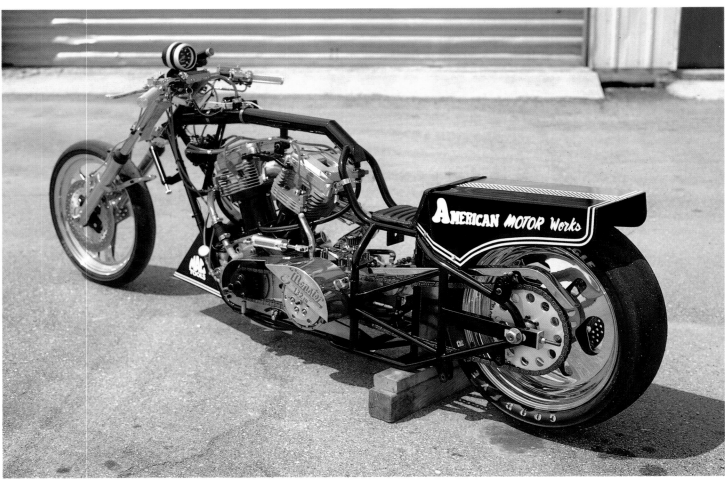

O fficially sanctioned drag racing has been one of the country's top spectator sports for many years. To remain competitive, the best machines have become increasingly complex. Packed with hardware from aftermarket manufacturers like S&S, Redshift, and J&E, the 80-cubic-inch engine has been enlarged to a whopping 132 cubes—a 65-percent increase. The tubular frame was built by Bonnie Truett, whose creations have been run by top racers for years. A quarter-mile from the lights, stopping begins to gain in importance, a chore handled by Performance Machine anchors at both ends.

1. Harley-Davidson celebrated the 30th anniversary of the Electra Glide in 1995 with this special-edition FLHTCI. 2. First seen in the Sixties, "Davey" was re-released by the Testor Company in 1995. 3. This 1955 Chevy bank can help save up for a new Harley. 4. Many Harley diners have sprung up across the country, but the Gatto Cycle Diner in Tarentum, Pennsylvania, adjoins a Harley dealership.

1993 1994

Harley-Davidson celebrates its 90th anniversary in the summer of 1993 with a party in Milwaukee; festivities include a two-and-a-half-hour parade of Harleys through the city streets

The Harley mystique captivates a growing number of celebrities—and ex-foreign-bike riders

New models begin to sell out 12 months before they arrive in the showroom

An earthquake measuring 6.8 on the Richter scale hits Los Angeles in January of 1994

1. As it has become more socially acceptable, a greater number of families are enjoying the sport of motorcycling. 2. Sturgis, South Dakota, has been the home of the Black Hills Rally for better than 50 years, and continues to draw thousands of visitors every summer. 3. Women riders are becoming more common and now account for one of every four new Harleys sold. 4. You've probably wondered how good 'ol Saint Nick amuses himself in the off-season. He apparently keeps in practice by dispensing good cheer at Sturgis.

1

2

3

4

1. Customized motorcycles have often been considered rolling works of art, but few are more deserving of that title than this late-model Harley painted by world-renowned artist Leonardo Nierman. 2. At the other end of the spectrum are bikes that attract attention not because of their beauty, but rather their...uh...*individuality*. Known as "Rat bikes," the one carrying the most "trim" wins. This example is assured high marks at Daytona.

1994

1994 sees the return of Harley to racing as the VR1000 makes its debut—along with a limited run of street-legal versions

Due to a players strike, the World Series is cancelled in 1994 for the first time in 90 years

George Foreman, now 45, regains the heavyweight boxing title in November

1

2

3

1-2. Scott Jacobs is the only artist licensed by Harley-Davidson, and his work, though done on canvas, has an almost photographic quality to it. 3. Those who would like to "build" their own Harley piece-by-piece can now do so with this colorful puzzle.

1

2

1995 The Federal Building in
Oklahoma City is bombed
April 19, 1995; 169 are killed

In June, the U.S. space shuttle
Atlantis docks with the
Russian *MIR* space station

U.S. sends troops to Bosnia at
year's end

In 1995, total production tops
100,000 for the first time in
Harley history, 30 percent of
which is slated for export

Opposite page: 1. Introduced in 1990, the FLSTF Fat Boy has become a popular staple in the Big Twin line. It carried on for 1996 with its slim front fender and unique solid wheels. 2. Similar to the Fat Boy but wearing spoke wheels, whitewall tires, and skirted fenders was the FLSTN Heritage Softail Special. *This page:* 1. Bringing back the spirit of the old XLCH was the XL 1200S, a "sportier" Sportster. It carried special suspension, sport seat, and dual-disc front brakes. 2. The upscale full-size catalog for 1996 included a small vinyl record of "Road Music." 3. Topping the price spectrum was the FLHTC UI Ultra Classic Electra Glide with Sidecar. Some of the FLs offered fuel injection (noted by an "I" in the model designation), which brought with it a modest increase in power. 4. The FXD Dyna Super Glide was 1996's entry-level Big Twin.

© Harley-Davidson

1

2

Harley-Davidson reentered the racing scene in the Nineties with the water-cooled VR1000. As yet, however, the team has not been able to duplicate the success of the "Wrecking Crew" of the late Teens, nor has the VR1000 been as dominating a force as the WRs of the Fifties or the XRs of the Seventies. 1. Daytona Beach, 1994: The Harley garage is a beehive of activity as the crew readies the hardware for its first outing. 2. Miguel DuHamel was the pilot in the first season. 3. In order to qualify the VR1000 as a "production" racer, a limited number of street versions had to be built; note the headlight, turn signals, and mirrors. 4. DuHamel rounds a corner in Elkhart Lake, Wisconsin.

3

4

1. In its second year of campaigning, the VR1000 was fitted with a new dual-canister muffler in an effort to round up a few more horsepower. 2. Doug Chandler took over the reins for 1995. Here he's seen flinging the VR through turn five at Road America. 3. A well-restored Topper scooter makes for a handy way to get around the pits. Note that it's painted in Harley's racing colors: Black on one side, orange on the other, white in the middle, just like the VR1000. 4. A scale model of the VR1000 racer was released by Harley-Davidson in 1995, and sold well despite a $75 price tag. Note the single muffler, indicating it's based on the 1994 version.

1

2

3

4

1

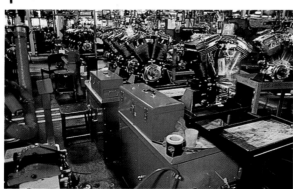

2

3

4

Harley-Davidson has adopted modern manufacturing techniques over the last decade or so that have helped to increase production efficiency. 1. VR1000s are built in a separate building by a small staff. 2. The engine-building facility is located in a suburb of Milwaukee, and features a highly automated system. 3. There are still some procedures better done by hand. Here some finishing touches are applied to an FLSTC. 4. These special Rotax-powered on/off road machines are built for the U.S. military.

1

2

While engines are still built near Milwaukee, final assembly takes place in York, Pennsylvania.
1. Engines arriving in York are readied for installation. 2. With engines and forks in place, these frames are beginning to take on the shape of a real motorcycle. 3. Awaiting only a few finishing touches, this FXDWG is nearly ready to be delivered to its eager—and soon to be proud—buyer. Production is scheduled to be increased for 1996 as demand is greatly exceeding supply; current waiting lists range from about six months for a Sportster to over two years for some of the more popular Big Twins.

3

1

2

3

1

2

3

4

5

6

Harley-Davidson has long attracted celebrity aficionados, but the current crop seems much more numerous and diverse than ever before. *Opposite page:* 1. Prior to achieving heartthrob status as a doctor on *ER*, George Clooney is shown kicking back on his hog. 2. Patrick Swayze straddles a Wide Glide. 3. Cher breaks out her Harley for a ride in a California parade in 1994. *This page:* 1. Actor Larry Hagman is a long-time Harley rider. 2. Pamela Anderson, recently of *Baywatch*, trades her Speedo for slightly more suitable motorcycling attire. 3. Musician Jon Bon Jovi lounges with his '89 Harley. 4. Actress Linda Hamilton looks right at home on her Harley. 5. Dean Cain, who plays Superman on *Lois and Clark*, sets out toward the wild blue yonder on a wild blue hog. 6. Shown astride his World War II-vintage WLA is Bob Collins, one of Chicago's best-known radio personalities.